Working Women

OPPOSING
VIEWPOINTS®

OTHER BOOKS OF RELATED INTEREST

Working Women

OPPOSING VIEWPOINTS®

David L. Bender, *Publisher*
Bruno Leone, *Executive Editor*
Brenda Stalcup, *Managing Editor*
Scott Barbour, *Senior Editor*
Mary E. Williams, *Book Editor*
Brenda Stalcup, *Assistant Editor*
Karin L. Swisher, *Assistant Editor*

OPPOSING
VIEWPOINTS®
SERIES

Greenhaven Press, Inc., San Diego, California

Cover photos: MetaTools

Library of Congress Cataloging-in-Publication Data

Working Women : opposing viewpoints / Mary E. Williams, book editor; Brenda Stalcup, Karin L. Swisher, assistant editors.
    p.   cm. — (Opposing viewpoints series)
  Includes bibliographical references and index.
  ISBN 1-56510-677-6 (lib. : alk. paper). —
ISBN 1-56510-676-8 (pbk. : alk. paper)
  1. Women—Employment. 2. Discrimination in employment.
3. Sex discrimination against women. 4. Sexual harassment of
women. 5. Women and the military. 6. Children of working mothers.
I. Williams, Mary E., 1960– . II. Stalcup, Brenda. III. Swisher, Karin,
1966– . IV. Series: Opposing viewpoints series (Unnumbered)
HD6053.W6773 1998
331.4—dc21   97-27517
                                                CIP

Every effort has been made to trace the owners of copyrighted material.

"CONGRESS SHALL MAKE NO LAW...ABRIDGING THE FREEDOM OF SPEECH, OR OF THE PRESS."

First Amendment to the U.S. Constitution

The basic foundation of our democracy is the First Amendment guarantee of freedom of expression. The Opposing Viewpoints Series is dedicated to the concept of this basic freedom and the idea that it is more important to practice it than to enshrine it.

CONTENTS

WHY CONSIDER OPPOSING VIEWPOINTS?

"The only way in which a human being can make some approach to knowing the whole of a subject is by hearing what can be said about it by persons of every variety of opinion and studying all modes in which it can be looked at by every character of mind. No wise man ever acquired his wisdom in any mode but this."

John Stuart Mill

In our media-intensive culture it is not difficult to find differing opinions. Thousands of newspapers and magazines and dozens of radio and television talk shows resound with differing points of view. The difficulty lies in deciding which opinion to agree with and which "experts" seem the most credible. The more inundated we become with differing opinions and claims, the more essential it is to hone critical reading and thinking skills to evaluate these ideas. Opposing Viewpoints books address this problem directly by presenting stimulating debates that can be used to enhance and teach these skills. The varied opinions contained in each book examine many different aspects of a single issue. While examining these conveniently edited opposing views, readers can develop critical thinking skills such as the ability to compare and contrast authors' credibility, facts, argumentation styles, use of persuasive techniques, and other stylistic tools. In short, the Opposing Viewpoints Series is an ideal way to attain the higher-level thinking and reading skills so essential in a culture of diverse and contradictory opinions.

In addition to providing a tool for critical thinking, Opposing Viewpoints books challenge readers to question their own strongly held opinions and assumptions. Most people form their opinions on the basis of upbringing, peer pressure, and personal, cultural, or professional bias. By reading carefully balanced opposing views, readers must directly confront new ideas as well as the opinions of those with whom they disagree. This is not to simplistically argue that everyone who reads opposing views will—or should—change his or her opinion. Instead, the series enhances readers' understanding of their own views by encouraging confrontation with opposing ideas. Careful examination of others' views can lead to the readers' understanding of the logical inconsistencies in their own opinions, perspective on

why they hold an opinion, and the consideration of the possibility that their opinion requires further evaluation.

EVALUATING OTHER OPINIONS

To ensure that this type of examination occurs, Opposing Viewpoints books present all types of opinions. Prominent spokespeople on different sides of each issue as well as well-known professionals from many disciplines challenge the reader. An additional goal of the series is to provide a forum for other, less known, or even unpopular viewpoints. The opinion of an ordinary person who has had to make the decision to cut off life support from a terminally ill relative, for example, may be just as valuable and provide just as much insight as a medical ethicist's professional opinion. The editors have two additional purposes in including these less known views. One, the editors encourage readers to respect others' opinions—even when not enhanced by professional credibility. It is only by reading or listening to and objectively evaluating others' ideas that one can determine whether they are worthy of consideration. Two, the inclusion of such viewpoints encourages the important critical thinking skill of objectively evaluating an author's credentials and bias. This evaluation will illuminate an author's reasons for taking a particular stance on an issue and will aid in readers' evaluation of the author's ideas.

As series editors of the Opposing Viewpoints Series, it is our hope that these books will give readers a deeper understanding of the issues debated and an appreciation of the complexity of even seemingly simple issues when good and honest people disagree. This awareness is particularly important in a democratic society such as ours in which people enter into public debate to determine the common good. Those with whom one disagrees should not be regarded as enemies but rather as people whose views deserve careful examination and may shed light on one's own.

Thomas Jefferson once said that "difference of opinion leads to inquiry, and inquiry to truth." Jefferson, a broadly educated man, argued that "if a nation expects to be ignorant and free . . . it expects what never was and never will be." As individuals and as a nation, it is imperative that we consider the opinions of others and examine them with skill and discernment. The Opposing Viewpoints Series is intended to help readers achieve this goal.

David L. Bender & Bruno Leone,
Series Editors

Greenhaven Press anthologies primarily consist of previously published material taken from a variety of sources, including periodicals, books, scholarly journals, newspapers, government documents, and position papers from private and public organizations. These original sources are often edited for length and to ensure their accessibility for a young adult audience. The anthology editors also change the original titles of these works in order to clearly present the main thesis of each viewpoint and to explicitly indicate the opinion presented in the viewpoint. These alterations are made in consideration of both the reading and comprehension levels of a young adult audience. Every effort is made to ensure that Greenhaven Press accurately reflects the original intent of the authors included in this anthology.

INTRODUCTION

"Women experience inequalities in pay [and promotions] at virtually every level of occupation and industry."

Ida L. Castro

"In almost every corner of the working world, equal opportunity and hard work have led to steady, impressive gains for women."

Laura A. Ingraham

The ways in which society has distributed work and status among men and women has changed over time. Early in human history, the fact that women gave birth and breastfed their babies brought about a division of labor between men and women in many cultures. Although several cultures existed in which men and women shared various tasks equally, in much of the world women took on most of the responsibility for child care while men labored to procure food and shelter. In early societies, such a division of tasks was not necessarily an indicator of lower status for women. But in later, more developed societies, men, who worked outside the home for wages, had more economic power than women, who mainly performed unpaid labor inside the home. A woman who worked at home attending to chores, family needs, and child care had to rely on someone else—typically a man—to earn the money for life's necessities.

By the middle of the twentieth century, the male breadwinner/female homemaker division of labor had become a matter of tradition and social convention in the United States, and girls were expected to grow up to become housewives and mothers. Those women who did have paid employment outside the home mostly worked as secretaries, nurses, housekeepers, elementary school teachers, and child care providers—low-wage occupations that were considered appropriate for women. The civil rights and women's rights movements of the 1960s and 1970s, however, broke down many barriers to female employment outside the home and in fields that had been previously reserved for men. In the last three decades of the twentieth century, large numbers of women entered the paid workforce. Today, at least 74 percent of American women between the ages of twenty-five and fifty-four are employed, and women make up 46 percent of the civilian workforce.

Despite this late twentieth-century influx of women into the workforce, many contend that women still face obstacles in the working world because of sex discrimination. Such discrimination, they claim, often takes the form of female segregation in low-status, low-wage positions with limited opportunities for career advancement. According to Barbara F. Reskin and Irene Padavic, the authors of *Women and Men at Work*, gender segregation in the workplace is the norm in American society: "Fewer than 10 percent of Americans have a coworker of the other sex who does the same job, for the same employer, in the same location, and on the same shift." Furthermore, they maintain, "women are concentrated at low levels in the organizations that employ them and in the lower ranks in their occupations and professions," while men continue to be predominant in the higher-paying ranks of business, medicine, engineering, architecture, the military, and the legal fields. Rochelle Sharpe, a *Wall Street Journal* staff reporter, agrees, pointing out that women hold only one-fourth of the supervisory jobs and less than 5 percent of the senior management positions in the nation's largest companies. Moreover, many analysts assert, on average women earn only 72 percent of what men earn for doing the same work.

A number of commentators argue that disparities between men's and women's pay and promotions are the result of negative stereotypes about women and of male workers' indifference or opposition to women's advancement. Common stereotypes about women, they claim, include the assumptions that women are weak, passive, illogical, and in need of protection. Many contend that these assumptions, which are often unconscious, can affect workplace behavior and limit women's progress. For example, as Reskin and Padavic point out, if a male store manager assumes that a female clerk is especially vulnerable to crime and would be afraid to work at night, he will not consider promoting her to night manager. Others maintain, moreover, that since men often see women as threats to their privileged positions in the workplace, they deliberately hamper women's progress. According to Sharpe, "Women say they are ignored, not taken seriously and shunted into support jobs far from [a] company's core business, where there is little chance [for advancement]." In effect, these authorities conclude, both subtle and overt forms of sex discrimination are hindrances to working women's success.

Others disagree with the contention that sex discrimination is a serious problem for working women. They maintain that much of the disparity in wages and promotions between male and female workers results not from discrimination but from women's preference for lower-paying careers. Syndicated columnist Stephen Chapman notes that "men are more likely to get . . . degrees in engineering and business, while women are more drawn to education, English literature and communications. Engineers, whatever their sex, generally earn a lot more than teachers, whatever their sex." Furthermore, many authorities point out, women who become mothers often choose to take time off from work or to work shorter hours than men do. Because these women spend less time in the career track relative to their male counterparts, experts claim, they are less likely than men to build up the length of service required for raises and promotions.

Some policy analysts criticize the information-gathering methods of researchers who have concluded that women face workplace discrimination. For example, Diana Furchtgott-Roth of the American Enterprise Institute claims that the contention that women comprise only 5 percent of top-level managers is misleading. "Rather than comparing the number of women qualified to hold top positions with those who actually hold jobs," she states, "[researchers] compared the number of women in the labor force, without reference to experience or education levels, with those wielding power in top corporations." In reality, Furchtgott-Roth argues, there are very few women who are qualified for senior management positions. Most of these positions require advanced degrees and at least twenty-five years of work experience, she contends, and women in general do not yet have those degrees or years of experience because they have not been in the professional workforce long enough. However, a national survey reveals that among childless people twenty-seven to thirty-three years old, women's earnings were about 98 percent of men's. Such results, many authorities claim, suggest that working women have reached near parity with working men and are therefore not limited by sex discrimination.

The question of sex discrimination and other controversies surrounding women's increased participation in the workforce are addressed in the following chapters of *Working Women: Opposing Viewpoints*: What Are the Effects of Women's Increased Participation in the Workforce? How Serious Is Discrimination Against Female Workers? How Serious a Problem Is Sexual Harassment in the Workplace? Should Women Serve in the Military? These debates promise to intensify as women continue to enter professions traditionally occupied by men.

CHAPTER 1

WHAT ARE THE EFFECTS OF WOMEN'S INCREASED PARTICIPATION IN THE WORKFORCE?

CHAPTER PREFACE

Unprecedented numbers of women entered the paid labor force during the last three decades of the twentieth century. Many of these women were mothers. Government statistics from 1997 show that 62.3 percent of mothers with preschool-age children work outside the home either part- or full-time. Most of these women place their children in someone else's care while they are working: Day care centers or informal arrangements at the homes of relatives or friends are two common child care options. In response to this increased reliance on day care, psychologists, social scientists, and family researchers have drawn various conclusions about the effects of day care on children's development and well-being.

Some experts argue that a solid mother-infant attachment is necessary for a child's healthy emotional development. They contend that day care disrupts this crucial bond, resulting in behavioral problems and long-term emotional impairment in children. According to Brenda Hunter, a psychologist specializing in parent-infant attachment, babies placed in nonparental care for more than twenty hours a week are at risk for developing social and behavioral problems later in life. She maintains that many of the nation's social ills—including poor academic performance and rising rates of crime and suicide among young people—stem in part from unstable mother-infant attachments due to the use of day care.

Others contend that day care can actually benefit children. For example, a study conducted by the National Institute of Child Health and Human Development found that high-quality day care—most frequently provided by large child care centers—enhances children's intellectual development and improves the quality of mother-child relationships. Furthermore, the study revealed that the state of a child's family life, not the particular day care situation, was the most important factor determining a child's emotional health. If a mother frequently talks to and interacts with her baby, "the child is more likely to develop strong maternal bonds and a solid cognitive foundation, irrespective of the child's day care situation," these researchers state.

The effect of day care on children is among the issues discussed in the following chapter on the impact of the increasing number of working women.

"This dramatic movement of mothers
into the work force ... has exacted a
substantial, if still undetermined,
toll both on individual women and
society."

WOMEN'S INCREASED PARTICIPATION IN THE WORKFORCE HAS HARMED SOCIETY

Linda Chavez

The influx of women into the workforce during the last three
decades of the twentieth century has not benefited families or
society, asserts Linda Chavez in the following viewpoint. She
maintains that the feminist revolution of the 1960s, which led
to an increase in the number of working women, also contributed to the decline in family stability and the belief that
women should perform the same roles as men. This denial of
male-female difference, she concludes, has damaged men's sense
of masculinity and has discouraged them from fulfilling their
role as protectors of women and children. Chavez is John M.
Olin Fellow at the Manhattan Institute, a public policy organization in New York City.

As you read, consider the following questions:

1. What percentage of women with children under the age of
   eighteen work outside the home, according to Chavez?
2. Why do women feel pressure to work outside the home, in
   the author's opinion?
3. According to Chavez, what are feminists doing to mitigate
   the results of their revolution?

From Linda Chavez, "Emasculating Men," Crisis, June 1994. Reprinted by permission of
The Morley Institute, publisher of Crisis, Washington, D.C. To subscribe call 1-800-852-
9962 or visit www.crisismagazine.com.

The feminist revolution of the 1960s promised to liberate women from the overbearing protection of society, the constraints of traditional morality, the oppression of men, the burden of children. It has largely accomplished its mission in one of the most radical and rapid restructurings of society in history. But at what cost? Women are now free to work the same long hours, to do the same heavy lifting, in the same dangerous jobs as men. Women are free to have sex with as many partners as they choose with as little commitment as possible. They need not be vexed by fathers who want to safeguard their virtue, or brothers who would defend it. They are free not to marry at all; or leave their husbands (or, more often, be left by them) with virtually no legal hassle or consequent social stigma. They are free not to bear children or, in a perverse corollary, to bear them outside marriage.

THE FAMILY IS IN DECLINE

None of this sounds much like real freedom, however. Indeed, in the aftermath of the social revolution of the 1960s, women seem more burdened and vulnerable than free. The family, which historically has been the primary social unit that both protected women and gave them unique status, is in decline. An estimated 40 percent of married women in their 30s and 40s will divorce, and fewer women, especially black women, are marrying in the first place. The number of families headed by single women now stands at 12 percent overall and 46 percent among blacks. Those women who do marry have seen their role in the family redefined. A shrinking number, for example, find the financial security and emotional support to stay at home to raise their children. A large majority—68 percent—of women with children under 18 now work outside the home, including 60 percent of married women with children under six. In 1960, fewer than 20 percent of married women with pre-school aged children worked. Although feminists point to this dramatic movement of mothers into the work force as the crowning achievement of women's liberation, in fact it has exacted a substantial, if still undetermined, toll both on individual women and society. A majority of working mothers of young children, in fact, routinely tell pollsters that they would like either not to work at all or to work part-time while their children are young. But most feel they cannot make those choices.

Conventional wisdom suggests that declining real wages make two incomes necessary to support a middle-class lifestyle for most young couples, but part of the problem may be the constantly expanding definition of what constitutes a middle-class life. People believe they need more than they did in the past: bigger houses with more bedrooms, bathrooms, and amenities, including central air conditioning, microwave ovens, VCRs, color televisions; more and better-equipped cars; frequent lunches and dinners out. What were once defined as luxuries are now thought to be necessities. But economics aren't the only thing pressuring women to work outside the home. The social expectation that women will work—even after they marry and have children—is as great today as it once was that they would remain home with their children.

IDENTICAL ROLES FOR MEN AND WOMEN?

I recently asked a group of approximately one hundred students at a Catholic college about their anticipations in this regard. Only a handful of young women said that they planned to stay at home full time while their children were young. What was more surprising was that *none* of the young men in the audience said they would prefer their future wives to stay at home after the birth of their children. Indeed, my discussions with students suggest that most young men, especially those who are best educated, feel that it would be an unfair burden for them to assume the sole financial responsibility for their families; most seek to marry young women who will be, ideally, equal financial partners.

Reprinted by special permission of United Feature Syndicate.

Women no longer have any special status in this society. They are not only men's equals, they are expected to be their clones. At every turn, we insist on the essential sameness of men and women. We persist in the belief that men and women should fulfill identical roles in society. We demand not only equal pay for equal work for women, but also that women can and should perform the same jobs as men, including most recently—and outrageously—serving in combat. We deny that being a mother is different from being a father in any but a strictly biological sense, and we increasingly prefer to use the androgynous term "parent" to describe both roles. The very idea that sex roles are anything more than a social construct is anathema.

SECOND THOUGHTS

Yet, there are some signs that even the feminist movement is having second thoughts about the consequences of their revolution. Much of the recent spate of feminist legislation, for example, aims at ameliorating the effects of the social upheaval they have wrought over the last three decades. Parental leave laws will allow women to stay at home to care for newborn or sick children or other family members without risking their jobs. Vigorous enforcement of child support laws will mitigate the effect of divorce and abandonment, forcing men to remain financially—if not emotionally—tied to their children. And sexual harassment and date rape laws will attempt to keep men's behavior in check, while preserving women's right to exercise their own newly acquired sexual freedom. Ironically, the same feminists who wiped out the protective legislation of an earlier era now seek to impose a whole new generation of protective laws.

The feminists' solution to female vulnerability is to replace the role that men have traditionally played in women's lives—that of provider and protector—with government. It is as if the feminists are quietly conceding that they have failed in masculinizing women to be totally self-sufficient. But the real problem is that the feminist revolution has emasculated all too many men, who no longer wish to care for or protect women or their children. The result is not a kinder, gentler, feminized world, but rather one which reflects a pre-civilized and amoral state of nature, where the strong prey upon the weak, and women and their children are left out in the cold.

"For women, paid employment has resulted in heightened self esteem and improved physical and mental health."

WOMEN'S INCREASED PARTICIPATION IN THE WORKFORCE HAS BENEFITED SOCIETY

Caryl Rivers and Rosalind C. Barnett

In the following viewpoint, Caryl Rivers and Rosalind C. Barnett contend that the growing amount of women in the workforce has been beneficial. Employment improves the health and self-esteem of women, the authors maintain. Moreover, they assert, dual-income couples provide financial security and stable home environments for their children. Policymakers should therefore support working women and two-career families, they conclude. Barnett is a psychologist and senior research associate at the Wellesley College Center for Research on Women. Rivers is a journalism professor at Boston College. They are also the authors of *She Works, He Works: How Two-Income Families Are Happier, Healthier, and Better Off.*

As you read, consider the following questions:
1. According to the authors, when do working parents find time to spend with their children?
2. What percentage of household chores are done by women in two-earner couples, according to Rivers and Barnett?
3. In the authors' opinion, how could the condition of the economy harm working families?

From Caryl Rivers and Rosalind C. Barnett, "Just What Family Values Are 'Normal'?" *San Diego Union-Tribune*, editorial, August 16, 1996. Reprinted by permission of the authors.

"**F**amily values" is turning into a hot political topic, with both Republicans and Democrats wrestling over who has the best policies and programs—and the best sound bites. But the truth about the American family is much different from the political TV spots and news reports.

Almost daily, headlines trumpet the somber facts about the family. It's in "decline," with working parents frazzled wrecks and their kids prime candidates for psychiatrists' couches.

But the truth is quite different, as evidenced by a major study of American couples who are employed full time. The study was funded by a million-dollar grant from the National Institute of Mental Health (NIMH).

Contrary to myth, these couples are coping well with their often-stressful lives, with a low incidence of anxiety and depression, and few physical symptoms of the sort that accompany stress-related illness. They report warm relations with their children, and that their children are thriving.

WHAT THE RESEARCH SHOWS

The NIMH research explodes a number of myths about the new American family:

• Myth: Moving away from the *Ozzie and Harriet* family—breadwinner father and homemaker mom—spells disaster.

Fact: Two-earner couples, even in tough times, were not facing anxiety over finances. While families with a single breadwinner could be plunged into economic chaos by the loss of a job, these couples have a safety net because of their dual incomes. Their lifestyle is a good fit with today's economic reality.

• Myth: Parents who work full time are too busy to care for their kids.

Fact: One study found that working parents spend as much time with their children as parents where one partner is not employed—but they do it on weekends and in evenings.

• Myth: Today's fathers can't compare with the wonderful dads of the *Father Knows Best* days.

Fact: Fathers in dual-earner couples spend much more time with their kids than '50s' fathers did. By the time their kids reach school age, men spend as much time parenting as do their wives. The reality of the '50s was not that "father knew best," but that he often wasn't around very much. Studies of '50s' fathers showed they envied their wives' closeness with the kids.

• Myth: Working women and their children are wrecks.

Fact: For women, paid employment has resulted in heightened self esteem and improved physical and mental health. Scores of studies show that employed women are healthier than home-makers, and the scare stories about working women didn't come true. They are not dropping dead of heart attacks, nor are they dying earlier because of overwork. Paid work provides a buffer against depression and anxiety. As for their children, study after study shows no differences between children of working mothers and those of homemakers on any measures of child development.

Women Are the New Providers

A 1995 study by the Families and Work Institute titled "The New Providers" noted that even among employed women who are married, 48% provide half or more of family income. Almost one-fourth of working women who are married say they expect their jobs to provide more long-term financial security for their families than their partners' jobs, up from 9% in 1981.

"It's time to end the debate about whether women's employment hurts families and undermines their care-giving roles," the study says. Women feel keenly responsible for their families, and employment is a major way they meet that responsibility, the study says.

Sue Shellenbarger, *Wall Street Journal*, May 11, 1995.

• Myth: Women do it all on the "second shift" while balky men resist doing work around the home.

Fact: In two-earner couples, men and women are both doing considerable work around the home—55 percent for women, 45 percent for men. The days of the couch-potato dad are over.

• Myth: It's always best for mom to be home full time.

Fact: We add stress to today's parents' lives by insisting that the only "real" family is the '50s' model. If we encourage women to drop out of the labor force or settle for crummy part-time jobs, their risk of anxiety and depression increases. If men take second jobs or work much longer hours their stress will increase. Today's fathers see time with children as important to their lives, and men in our study showed heightened stress if their wives got to spend considerably more time with the children.

The 1950s Are Over

• Myth: Yesterday's parents were better parents.

Fact: These couples have a good chance to be better parents than those of the *Ozzie and Harriet* era. The women do not suffer the high anxiety and depression that women endured in those years, and the men seem more closely bonded to their kids.

• *Myth:* The old "Family Values" will bring back "Happy Days."

Fact: The 1950s are not coming back. Men's wages are flat or declining; good jobs are vanishing overseas, middle managers are being laid off. Those who believe the *Ozzie and Harriet* lifestyle is the only right one will be subject to stress, guilt and marital tensions.

Disturbing trends in the economy could harm working families, however. Downsizing—with fewer people asked to do more work, more contingent jobs with no benefits and no vacation time and the failure of a national health-care plan cut into the time working parents can spend with children or cause them more worry.

The answer to these problems is not to pretend that one wage can support a family or to track women into low-paying, part-time jobs which offer high stress, no benefits and little sense of control or challenge. Research shows that bad jobs have a negative impact on the quality of parenting. Sixty-six percent of all families today are working families. Only when we accept working parents as "normal" parents can we create corporate and community policies that help and support these families.

"At a maquiladora plant . . . the young, female workers are allowed only two bathroom breaks a day, the drinking water is contaminated, and beatings and sexual abuse are commonplace."

SOME WORKING WOMEN ARE EXPLOITED BY FREE TRADE

Marc Breslow

Factories in Latin American free trade zones that produce cheap goods for companies in other countries often exploit women workers, contends Marc Breslow in the following viewpoint. He maintains that these factories—known as maquiladoras—offer meager wages and subject women to long work hours, unhealthy work environments, and physical and sexual abuse. This viewpoint includes an interview of Judith Viera and Claudia Molina, two former maquiladora workers from Central America, conducted by Karen Kampworth of the Committee in Solidarity with the People of El Salvador. Breslow is an editor for the progressive journal *Dollars and Sense*.

As you read, consider the following questions:

1. According to Breslow, which popular U.S. retailers buy goods from Central American maquiladoras?
2. How does Viera describe the work schedule at the factory where she was employed?
3. What happened at the El Salvadoran maquiladora when the workers tried to form a union, according to Viera?

From Marc Breslow, "Crimes of Fashion: Those Who Suffer to Bring You GAP T-Shirts," *Dollars & Sense*, November/December 1995. Reprinted by permission. *Dollars & Sense* is a progressive economics magazine published ten times a year. First-year subscriptions cost $16.95 and may be ordered by writing *Dollars & Sense*, One Summer St., Somerville, MA 02143 or calling 617-628-2025.

At a maquiladora plant owned by Mandarin International in El Salvador, Judith Viera earned $43 for working an 88-hour week. Conditions were horrific: the young, female workers are allowed only two bathroom breaks a day, the drinking water is contaminated, and beatings and sexual abuse are commonplace. When Viera and her co-workers tried to improve conditions by organizing a union, the company responded with violence and mass firings.

Mandarin sells to the Gap and Eddie Bauer, among other U.S. firms. Its plant can produce 1,500 Gap t-shirts a day, which sell for $20 each in the United States—while the maquiladora workers are paid 16 cents per shirt. By not owning Mandarin and similar factories, the Gap and other retailers avoid direct responsibility for pitiful wages and abusive conditions.

Meanwhile, in 1994 the Gap made $311 million in profits from its 1,300 stores throughout the United States and Canada. And Gap CEO Donald Fisher paid himself $2 million, not including stock options.

CHEATING WOMEN WORKERS

The Gap is not alone. Other popular U.S. retailers also buy from maquila firms in El Salvador, Honduras, Guatemala, and elsewhere. Gabo, for example, a Korean-owned plant also in El Salvador, sells to Marshall's, Sears, Wal-Mart, and Nordstrom's. Not only are the wages meager, but the company often cheats the women workers on their paychecks. In addition, while collecting social security taxes from its employees, Gabo regularly fails to give the money to the government, preventing the women from receiving free health care.

In July 1995 the National Labor Committee, a union-backed group in New York City that seeks to improve conditions at "maquila" plants in Central America, brought Judith Viera and Claudia Molina (from Honduras), to various U.S. cities to share their stories. The Committee pointed out that the conditions at Mandarin and other plants violate the Gap's own "code of conduct" for the factories it buys from.

This code sounds impressive, requiring, for example, that employers "must never force employees to work extra hours" and "may neither threaten nor penalize employees for their efforts to organize or bargain collectively." But the code of conduct is largely a public relations exercise, as the maquila owners violate it with impunity.

Responding to publicity from Viera and Molina's tour, the Gap issued a statement asserting that "we conduct thorough investigations of all new and potential vendors, and we strive hard to ensure that all business partners meet our sourcing guidelines—which set strict standards for working conditions and human rights." But the Gap claims not to have found any violations of its guidelines at Mandarin.

Charles Kernaghan, director of the Labor Committee, visited El Salvador's free trade zone in September. "We reached fifty of the workers who were fired, and interviewed them in groups. They confirmed what Judith Viera said," reports Kernaghan. Meanwhile, the maquila owners are trying to ensure that no other such stories reach the outside world. "There are armed guards everywhere, with sawed-off shotguns," Kernaghan says. And the women employees have been warned not to talk with any *gringos* who come around asking questions, or they will lose their jobs.

Viera and Molina can speak best for themselves. On July 14, 1995, they were interviewed in Boston by Karen Kampworth of the Committee in Solidarity with the People of El Salvador (CISPES). Below we provide excerpts from that interview, which was translated by Holly Grant, also of CISPES.

SURVIVING THE MAQUILAS

Viera: I am eighteen years old and am from El Salvador. In San Salvador my family lives in San Miguel. I have no father and my mother couldn't manage with all of us, so I only studied up until fifth grade. I worked one year in the maquila, where I learned a lot but suffered a lot of mistreatment.

Molina: I am seventeen years old and from Honduras. I worked in the maquila. My family is from Comayagua and Copan. I also only studied up to fifth grade. I also don't have a father and my mother couldn't handle schooling and the food and all.

Viera: We decided to work in the maquilas because it seemed like a nice job. Also we are minors, and I was only seventeen years old and only in a place like that was I able to work because I was underaged. In the maquilas there are girls who are fourteen, fifteen, and sixteen years old and only in a maquila can a fourteen-year old get a job.

Molina: I decided to work in a maquila because my mother earned very little money, and it wasn't enough for the food. I thought the job would be nice and easy, but it wasn't. I was only fifteen years old when I began working in the maquila.

Viera: I worked as "Secretary of the Line." I was in charge of everything that came in and left the factory line, all the completed shirts. I was in charge of controlling all the permissions, etc. of the people who worked in my line. I was in total charge of production of the line.

Molina: When I started I was a cutter and then I started working at the machines closing shirts. Then I worked making buttonholes and then cuffs. And then as punishment they moved me to packaging and made me work standing up. I did not like this work. But even though I didn't like the work, I had to do it because I needed the salary.

THE NATURE OF THE WORK

Kampworth: How many hours a day do you work?

Molina: I work thirteen hours a day and on Saturdays it is twenty-three hours of work.

Viera: My work schedule Monday to Thursday was from 7 am to 9 pm. On Fridays it was from 7 am to 5 pm, and then 7 pm to 3 am, and we stayed in the factory and slept on the floor to begin work again on Saturday from 7 am to 5 pm. For all that work the most I earned was 750 colones for two weeks, which is $43 a week.

Kampworth: Does the $43 per week cover your costs?

Viera: No. With that all you can buy is a little food and bus fare. I take two buses—one from my house to downtown, and then another one to the free trade zone. Our budget is a lot bigger than what we earn, than what our salaries are.

Viera: We brought some shirts that we make—from the Gap, and we also work with Eddie Bauer and other brands.

Molina: This is the shirt that we make for Orion, Gitano, Manhattan and other brands, but the brand that we work with the most is Manhattan.

THE NEED FOR A UNION

Kampworth: Who had the idea of forming a union?

Viera: The idea came from a woman who worked in quality control because there was a lot of mistreatment . . . when there was a meeting in the morning to announce that a union had been formed, at lunchtime the company closed its doors and wouldn't open them for us. That is when the work stoppage began so that they would accept the union. We are paid very little; they yell at us; they hit us with the shirts; we get a ticket to go to the bathroom—we only get two tickets a day and can only go for five minutes; they put us out in the sun and make us sweep all day under the sun. There are other punishments as well. They do not give us purified water but contaminated water to drink. So we decided to form a union and there was lots of support.

We were able to get the company to open again on Monday, but they have continued to mistreat us since that day, firing people, many threats.

Molina: In the maquila where I worked, there was also lots of mistreatment. They also didn't give us permission. One compañera on March 20, 1995, had to miscarry in the factory because they didn't give her permission to go to the doctor. She had asked for permission beginning at 9 am until 4 pm, when they [finally] gave her permission, but it was too late.

© Huck/Konopacki Labor Cartoons. Reprinted with permission.

Kampworth: Were you afraid to join the union?

Viera: No, because there are so many mistreatments that occur in the factory. I wasn't able to support many of the work stoppages because I was Secretary. . . . Many times I was in meetings at which they said they were going to close the factory for two months so they could get rid of the union. They have fired many pregnant women and minors. They have fired more than 350 people solely for the reason that they were members of the union. I was fired together with my two sisters because we were members of the union.

WORKERS ARE ABUSED

Kampworth: Why did you come on tour?

Viera: It is important to be here on tour representing all the working Salvadoran women in the factory, so many people. I know this tour is important and that they will accept the union, and that all the women will get their jobs back. Our idea is that the people in the United States help us and support our campaign. I don't completely know how they can help us, but I know they can and they will.

Viera: In the factory there is also sexual abuse. There is an ex-colonel that is director of personnel. Many times he asked me out, he followed me in his car. He told me that if I went out with him I wouldn't be fired. Also, this man hired men who were ex-combatants in the army; these men are only there to control our union. If you try to present them something or if they fire someone and you don't like it, these men will beat or hit you. Last week, there was a work stoppage at the factory because they had fired several pregnant women and union leaders. The National Civilian Police showed up to forcibly move them by hitting them and they forced us to stop the strike. They also captured our secretary general of the union; and they hit them and threatened them. The situation now is that the factory does not want to re-instate the pregnant women and the union leaders. There are many people who've been fired. The union leadership continues to fight about this, and the factory continues to threaten to close.

"The environment at the
[maquiladora] was better than the
environment at home and the
industries offered these women a step
up from more limited horizons."

WORKING WOMEN ARE NOT EXPLOITED BY FREE TRADE

Society

Many companies in the United States and elsewhere purchase goods produced by maquiladoras—factories situated in Latin American free trade zones. These factories have been criticized by some commentators because of reported exploitation and abuse of women workers. In the following viewpoint, the editors of *Society* contend that women working in assembly plants on the United States–Mexico border do not face maltreatment and victimization on the job. According to the *Society* editors, the first large study of maquiladora workers reveals that women employed in these factories do not suffer significant mental or physical health problems because of their work. In fact, the editors claim, maquiladoras offer their workers economic and social opportunities that are generally unavailable to women who are unemployed or who work in the service industries. *Society* is a bimonthly journal that specializes in social science issues.

As you read, consider the following questions:
1. According to the *Society* editors, what kind of coverage do maquiladoras generally receive in the media?
2. What are the differences between the work environments and the home environments of women employed at maquiladoras, according to *Society*?

Instead of the oppressive sweatshops portrayed in news reports, assembly plants on the United States–Mexico border may actually improve the lives of the young Mexican women working in the plants, known as *maquiladora* industries. No adverse health effects from working in electronic and garment assembly plants in Tijuana, Mexico, were found in the first large controlled study of *maquiladora* workers, conducted through the University of California Berkeley's School of Public Health. Women who worked in electronics plants in Tijuana reported fewer physical impairments and less depression than women from the same communities who worked in non-industrial service jobs, according to the study of 480 women headed by Sylvia Guendelman, assistant professor of public health at U.C.-Berkeley.

Perhaps it is time, says Guendelman, to "stop treating *maquiladoras* as the 'ugly ducklings' of the new Mexican industrialization phase."

BORDER INDUSTRIES

The findings, published in the *American Journal of Public Health*, are particularly relevant in light of the North American Free Trade Agreement (NAFTA), which is expected to affect labor conditions and accelerate growth of the border industries. News reports on these industries often focus on adverse working conditions such as poor ventilation, lack of rest periods, excessive noise levels, long hours of detailed routine work, and exposure to toxic chemicals.

The Guendelman study challenges this perspective. It points to the relative nature of health effects and demonstrates that health is strongly influenced by subjective factors such as attitude toward work. In this case, the women were satisfied with their work, perhaps because the environment at the plant was better than the environment at home and the industries offered these women a step up from more limited horizons, said Guendelman.

FACTORY WORK OFFERS OPPORTUNITIES

Border assembly plants, which now number almost 2,200, employ more than 560,000 workers. Although they have been in operation since the 1960s, their rapid growth since 1982 in cities like Tijuana has caused a population explosion in the area. Entire new shanty towns have sprung up to house and supply the workforce. The towns have few resources, though, and often lack adequate sewage disposal, water supply, electricity, or telephone lines. By comparison, the work environment at the assembly plants looks good, says Guendelman. The factories offer cafeterias, social hours, Friday night barbecues, volleyball games, picnics, and air conditioning.

"Going to work is a social event for the women," says Guendelman, "it gives them an opportunity to be among other co-workers and to enjoy a good meal."

Factory work also provides an economic alternative to early marriage and child rearing or low-level service jobs. Guendelman quickly adds, though, that the work is monotonous, mechanical, and high-pressure.

FINDINGS OF THE STUDY

The Guendelman study is the first to compare industrial work with other options open to Mexican women from the same communities. The women in the study were placed in four groups: electronic and garment workers (two sectors of the maquiladora industry), service workers (housekeepers, waitresses, and school teachers), and non-wage earners. Compared to service jobs, work on the assembly line was worse in several respects. Although fringe benefits and bonuses were better, the assembly work paid lower wages on the average. The women worked longer hours and had less control over their work.

BENEFITS FOR EVERYONE

Maquiladoras operate on a simple principle: You can ship your raw materials and parts from the U.S. to Mexico, where they will be processed by low-cost Mexican labor and returned to the U.S. as finished or semifinished products, paying customs duties only on the non-U.S. portion of the product. For Mexico it is a way of earning foreign exchange by exporting labor without exporting laborers. For poor Mexicans it is a way of making a decent living without having to brave U.S. border patrols. For U.S. manufacturers it is a way to stay world competitive without having to move their entire operations abroad.

Christopher Palmeri, Forbes, February 13, 1995.

However, the study did not find more frequent cases of backaches, joint pains, respiratory problems, stomach aches, or other health problems among assembly line workers than among the women in other occupations. In fact, electronics workers reported fewer functional impediments than did the women in the other three groups. They also had the lowest rates of mental depression. Garment workers, however, were found to be in poorer health than women working in electronics assembly plants.

All four groups of women workers had high stress scores on the control scale, indicating a low sense of control over their lives. They also had high depression scores compared to a U.S. standard, but these results are difficult to interpret in a cross-cultural context, said Guendelman. On global measures of satisfaction most of the women in all three work sectors described themselves as satisfied with their work and their lives.

Variation on the work satisfaction scale—which was influenced by relationships with co-workers and managers—turned out to be one of the few predictors of health outcome in the study. Those who ranked themselves as unhappy or dissatisfied with the work, particularly with their work relationships, had poorer health. These results must be viewed with caution, however, since the women were young (generally between the ages of sixteen and twenty-eight) and healthy to begin with. Additional studies would have to be done to determine chronic effects and possible reproductive hazards.

"Children do not flourish in the empty house."

MOTHERS' PARTICIPATION IN THE WORKFORCE HARMS CHILDREN

Brenda Hunter, interviewed by Jill Zook-Jones

In the following viewpoint, Brenda Hunter maintains that children's social and psychological growth can be damaged by their working mothers' absence from home. Moreover, she contends, a majority of working mothers would actually prefer to spend more time at home because they recognize how important their presence is to their children. In her opinion, stay-at-home mothers deserve support because consistent maternal care is crucial to a child's sense of security and long-term emotional development. Hunter, a psychologist and specialist in infant attachment, is author of *Home by Choice* and *What Every Mother Needs to Know*. She is interviewed by freelance writer Jill Zook-Jones.

As you read, consider the following questions:

1. In the author's opinion, why has motherhood been belittled in America?
2. What percentage of mothers would prefer to spend more time at home with their children, according to Hunter?
3. In Hunter's opinion, why is maternal love especially important for infants?

From "The Maternal Imperative" by Brenda Hunter, interviewed by Jill Zook-Jones, *Christianity Today*, March 7, 1994. Reprinted with permission.

Jill Zook-Jones: *You argue in your book* Home by Choice *that our current cultural climate is hostile to "mother love." What do you mean?*

Brenda Hunter: Our culture tells mothers they are not that important in their children's lives. For three decades, mothering has been devalued in America. It has even become a status symbol for the modern woman to take as little time as possible away from work for full-time mothering.

I believe it started in the 1960s. We can't blame everything on radical feminists, but some of them suggested that work in the office would take care of women's angst. In the 1980s, we saw the emergence of the myth that anyone could care for a mother's children as well as Mother herself. And in the 1990s, we hear that fathers are unnecessary, that children thrive in any family setting, whether it be homosexual or single-parent.

"Dan Quayle Was Right," the much-discussed article in the April 1993 *Atlantic* by Barbara Dafoe Whitehead, stated that children do better in intact, two-parent families. Unfortunately, we've made it too costly psychologically for many women to take time out from careers and stay home with their child.

What kind of cost do you see?

The mother at home is either forgotten in the secular media or she is denigrated. During Mother's Day weekend in 1993, I read the *Washington Post* and *USA Weekend*, and most of the articles in one way or another put down the mother at home. On that day, at least one national daily chose to say that the mental health of housewives was poorer than the mental health of employed mothers. It's not a happy image for mothers who are struggling with little kids.

THE PREFERENCE FOR HOME

Then why are more mothers staying home, as you point out in Home by Choice?

In 1990, for the first time since 1948, the number of women in the work force dropped. Also in 1990, the birth rate rose 10.5 percent from 1980. In 1990 the Roper Organization found that for the first time since 1980, the majority of women polled—51 percent—said they preferred to stay home. Poll after poll indicates that about two-thirds of mothers would prefer to spend more time home with their children if money were not a problem.

I've heard from mothers across America whose hearts are home even if their bodies are at the office. Some say, "I'm not home now but I will be in six months," or "after my second child is born." After I was on the *Today* show on a Saturday, over

100 mothers called, inquiring about working from home.

Don't mothers find support in the church?

I hear younger women saying all the time, "Where are the older mothers? Grandma's on a career track or on a cruise. Where is the kind of woman mentioned in Titus 2 who can help me with my life?"

Fortunately, some churches are starting mentoring programs. As a psychologist, I know that women are better wives and mothers if they have sufficient emotional support.

THE MOTHER-CHILD RELATIONSHIP

You argue that the issue is more than one of modeling or getting training in parenting techniques, but of healthy patterns of intimacy established in infancy. What do you mean?

The eminent British psychiatrist John Bowlby believes that a baby's emotional bond or attachment to his mother is the foundation stone of personality. If my parents are emotionally accessible and they love me, I feel loved and worthy. If not, I feel unloved and unworthy. That in turn affects my ability to be emotionally accessible to my children in adulthood.

INFANT ATTACHMENT THEORY

The attachment theory predicts that babies are at risk psychologically if separated from their mothers for twenty or more hours per week during their first twelve months of life. Years of experiments by other researchers have proven that fifty percent of daycare babies are insecurely attached to their mothers. Incidentally, this situation applies not only to center-based daycare, but to other forms of non-maternal care as well. Children from affluent homes cared for by nannies still displayed significant insecurity in their attachments.

Mary Monica, Fidelity, July/August 1993.

But is maternal deprivation more damaging than paternal neglect?

That's hard to answer. And I believe that mothers and fathers are equally important. I do not believe they are interchangeable. But I believe that mothers and fathers do different things for children. Children learn to be intimate primarily from their mothers in that early maternal relationship. Sigmund Freud emphasized the singular importance of the mother or mother figure in the child's early life as "unique, without parallel . . . as the prototype of all later love relationships for both sexes." I believe that Mother is very much the architect of intimacy. Cross-culturally, infancy seems to belong to mothers.

What about the mother who feels emotionally unequipped for parenting? Is it better for the child for her to be home?

Women who stay home need to keep the intellectual life alive. I'm not trying to put people on a guilt trip. But I suggest that there are many things a mother who stays at home can do to thrive. If a mother is depressed at home, she may need to recognize that there is an absence of nurture in her past and work through this pain through psychotherapy or nurturing relationships with older women. Some in the mental health profession have discovered that older women can provide an invaluable resource to younger, struggling mothers. Why the church doesn't do more with this is a mystery to me.

MOTHERS ARE NEEDED IN THE HOME

If children need accessible parents, when does that need stop?

Obviously children of school age need less time with their mothers than babies and children. That's why I encourage women to develop their gifts at home. Lots of women go back to work. If they can have a full-time job that lets them off after school, great. I'm big on at-home careers; what I am against is the empty house. Children do not flourish in the empty house. I once heard an authority on teen pregnancy say that usually a girl has her first sexual experience in her or her boyfriend's empty house.

Newsweek said there are some 10 million latchkey children in this country. I was a latchkey child. I know what it feels like. I know about the fear of the burglar. I used to look under the beds and check the closets every day when I came home. And I felt lonely. Having my mother telephone and say, "How are you?" helped, but a phone call is no substitute for a mother's presence.

My girls were in high school when I went back to school for my doctorate. I had an experimental psychology lab late in the afternoon twice a week. I didn't think my girls would notice. But I remember Holly—a high-school senior—commenting several times that she missed me. It was important for me to be there to talk to and have a cup of tea with my teens after school.

CHILDREN ARE A PRIORITY

What's at stake in all this?

We have to put it into a larger, cultural perspective. I recently reread *Brave New World* by Aldous Huxley, and it was frightening. When we weaken attachments between parents and children, all kinds of anomalies occur, as Huxley showed. We're headed there. In the book *Generations,* William Strauss and Neil Howe argue that the twentysomething generation has the highest incidence of maternal employment and parental divorce of any American generation. It's also the most aborted generation. It has the highest rate of incarceration and the second-highest suicide rate. Moreover, I believe we already have a daycare generation among us, and we're working on another.

So I appeal to parents and churches and ask, What about the children? In our career pursuits—mothers and fathers—let's not forget them. Our lifestyles as mothers may have changed, but our children's needs are the same.

> "We need to become more skeptical of 'expert' advice on child rearing, especially when that advice sets impossible standards for mothers."

MOTHERS' PARTICIPATION IN THE WORKFORCE DOES NOT HARM CHILDREN

Diane Eyer

Diane Eyer, author of *Mother-Infant Bonding: A Scientific Fiction*, teaches psychology at the University of Pennsylvania in Philadelphia. In the following viewpoint, she argues that children are not harmed by daily separation from mothers who work outside the home. The theory that infants and young children must bond with stay-at-home mothers to develop normally has no basis in scientific fact, Eyer contends. She maintains that such theories wrongly blame working mothers for society's ills.

As you read, consider the following questions:

1. According to Eyer, in what ways was the initial study on mother-infant bonding flawed?
2. How did the theory on mother-infant bonding become accepted as fact, according to the author?
3. In Eyer's opinion, what helps children prosper?

From Diane Eyer, Viewpoint, "Is Mother-Infant Bonding a Myth?" *Glamour*, July 1993. Reprinted by permission of Sanford J. Greenburger & Associates, as agents for the author.

Jennifer returned to work six weeks after her daughter was born. Some of her friends expressed surprise: "Don't you worry that you won't bond properly with Steffie?" one of them asked. Another said she'd heard that if mothers don't spend enough time with their infants in the first few months, the babies never become securely "attached." Now Jennifer is wondering whether she should leave her job to spend more time with her daughter. But she'd still have to work part-time; she and her husband need a second income. Would mornings at home be enough to ensure that Steffie wouldn't grow up with some sort of problem?

MOTHER-INFANT BONDING IS A MYTH

Jennifer will never be able to spend enough time with her new baby to bond successfully—because mother-infant bonding is a myth. There are a dozen different definitions of bonding, none of which have any valid scientific basis. Yet pediatric experts have been arguing for more than a decade that bonding, often defined as something best guaranteed by stay-at-home mothering in the first year of life, is critical to a child's future mental health and school performance. Noted child-rearing expert T. Berry Brazelton has even suggested that children who fail to bond with parents before the age of one may grow up to be terrorists.

The theory of bonding was developed in the early 1970s, when a study appeared to show that women who had 16 extra hours of contact over a few days with their new babies became better mothers. The researchers hypothesized that for a short time after giving birth women are hormonally "primed" to accept their infants; if they fail to take advantage of this window of opportunity, they might later reject their babies. As further "proof" of bonding, the researchers pointed to female goats, who if separated from their new offspring for as little as five minutes will thereafter ignore them. Soon, "failure to bond" was being used to explain why many of the babies who were separated from their mothers in neonatal intensive-care units were later abused or neglected by their families.

Not only was this analogy between women and goats shaky (most animals do not abandon their young after a separation), but the study itself was very limited—it included only 28 women—and poorly designed. Amazingly, the researchers never even measured the women's hormone levels to establish that a postpartum priming period actually exists. And the definition of better mothering was dubious. For example, the mothers were asked, "Have you been out since the baby was born?" Mothers who said no got the highest "good mothering" scores. They also received high scores if they stood close to the examining table during a pediatric exam one month after the birth. Was this better mothering or anxiety? Dozens of follow-up studies on bonding conducted between the early 1970s and the early 1980s, though they used bigger sample sizes, were similarly biased or badly designed.

EMPLOYED MOTHERS WERE JUST AS WARM

One intricate study brought 100 mother and child pairs into the laboratory and observed them as they played a cooperative game. The interactions were coded on a number of dimensions. The researchers rated the mothers on the extent to which they were accepting, protective, indulgent, and ready to discipline the child. The employed mothers were just as warm in their interactive style as the at-home mothers.

Faye J. Crosby, *Juggling: The Unexpected Advantages of Balancing Career and Home for Women and Their Families*, 1991.

How did such flimsy research become scientifically accepted fact, and from there a prescription for women to stay home for at least the first year of an infant's life? In large part, the notion of bonding took hold because it fit in neatly with an established prejudice among pediatricians: that a mother is the chief architect of her child's fate. In the 1940s, psychiatrist John Bowlby and psychoanalyst René Spitz put forth the notion of "maternal deprivation," arguing (on the basis of studies of children in extreme situations—for example, infants in foundling homes who had up to 50 different caretakers during their first months) that a child's contact with its biological mother during the first three years of life is crucial to its ability to form healthy relationships. In the 1950s, psychologists told women who wished to work outside the home that maternal deprivation would cause their children to become neurotics at best, sociopaths at worst. The women's movement temporarily dismantled such notions, but a backlash was inevitable. As women poured into the workplace throughout the 1970s, challenging men's power both at the office and in the home, bonding not so coincidentally became the hot new theory, reminding women that they alone were responsible for the fate of their children. When bonding seemed to be a matter of a few extra hours of contact after birth, many women jumped to embrace the theory: Here was a way to quickly ensure one's mothering success. But as bonding became defined as the work not of days but of months or years, it became a new source of pressure on mothers to abandon the workplace for home.

THE NEED FOR SKEPTICISM

For years, reliable studies have been telling us *not* that a child requires full-time care from a biological mother but that children generally thrive when they have good, stable relationships with several reasonably well-adjusted adults (and that adults are likely to be better adjusted when they have a life outside the home). The history of the bonding theory is a reminder that "scientific findings" sometimes become gospel despite their unsoundness. We need to become more skeptical of "expert" advice on child rearing, especially when that advice sets impossible standards for mothers or makes them scapegoats for all the complicated ills of our culture.

PERIODICAL BIBLIOGRAPHY

The following articles have been selected to supplement the diverse views presented in this chapter. Addresses are provided for periodicals not indexed in the *Readers' Guide to Periodical Literature*, the *Alternative Press Index*, the *Social Sciences Index*, or the *Index to Legal Periodicals and Books*.

Marian Burros	"Even Women at the Top Still Have Floors to Do," *New York Times*, May 31, 1993.
Kristin Droege	"Child Care: An Educational Perspective," *Jobs and Capital*, Winter 1995. Available from Milken Institute for Job & Capital Formation, 1250 Fourth Street, Second Floor, Santa Monica, CA 90401-1353.
Peter F. Drucker	"The Continuing Feminist Experiment," *Wall Street Journal*, October 17, 1994.
Elizabeth Fox-Genovese	"The State of Contemporary Politics and Culture," *Tikkun*, March/April 1994.
Nikki van der Gaag	"The Missing Billionairess," *New Internationalist*, September 1994.
Patricia Hedberg	"Get a Life—Lose a Job?" *Business Ethics*, September/October 1996.
Linda Himelstein	"Breaking Through," *Business Week*, February 17, 1997.
Michele Ingrassia	"Daughters of Murphy Brown," *Newsweek*, August 2, 1993.
Peter T. Kilborn	"More Women Take Low-Wage Jobs Just So Their Families Can Get By," *New York Times*, March 13, 1994.
Julia Lawlor	"Executive Exodus," *Working Woman*, November 1994.
Gretchen Morgenson	"I Didn't Know I Was Oppressed," *Forbes*, March 15, 1993.
Elena Neuman	"More Moms Are Homeward Bound," *Insight*, January 10, 1994. Available from 3600 New York Ave. NE, Washington, DC 20002.
Joan E. Rigdon	"A Wife's Higher Pay Can Test a Marriage," *Wall Street Journal*, January 28, 1993.

Andrea Sachs   "Desperately Seeking Daycare," *ABA Journal*,
                      June 1993.

Sue Shellenbarger   "Women Indicate Satisfaction with Role of Big
                      Breadwinner," *Wall Street Journal*, May 11, 1995.

Julie Gannon Shoop   "Working Mothers See Double Standard in
                      Custody Cases," *Trial*, October 1995.

Karen Stabiner   "A Suitable Mom," *Los Angeles Times Magazine*,
                      March 6, 1994. Available from Reprints, Times
                      Mirror Square, Los Angeles, CA 90053.

Paulette Thomas   "Women in Business: A Global Report Card,"
                      Wall Street Journal, July 26, 1995.

CHAPTER 2

HOW SERIOUS IS DISCRIMINATION AGAINST FEMALE WORKERS?

CHAPTER PREFACE

After the passage of the Civil Rights Act of 1964, affirmative action policies were implemented to correct the effects of discrimination on female and minority workers. These policies required employers to take active measures to achieve gender and racial diversity in the workplace—typically through programs designed to enlarge the pool of qualified female and minority job applicants. Today, however, some policymakers contend that affirmative action is no longer necessary because overt job discrimination has been effectively curtailed. Furthermore, many argue, affirmative action creates unfair hiring preferences for women.

According to these critics, affirmative action policies are a form of special treatment that gives women unmerited access to jobs. This practice causes male employees to resent successful female workers, opponents maintain, and it undermines female employees by suggesting that they need governmental sanctions to succeed. Attorney Laura Ingraham, for example, argues that affirmative action "creates animosity among men who are trying just as hard as their female counterparts to succeed . . . , as well as among women who do not want people thinking they got where they are because of affirmative action." Other commentators point to working women's success stories as proof that gender-based hiring preferences are unnecessary. According to syndicated columnist Stephen Chapman, "Women have made stunning gains in almost every field over the past generation. And . . . [they] have reached near-parity in wages and salaries."

Supporters of affirmative action policies argue that women continue to face discrimination in the workforce. In their opinion, these policies have allowed women to achieve some success in the workplace; however, they contend, significant gaps in income and professional status still exist between men and women. According to Marcia D. Greenberger, founder of the National Women's Law Center, "Women remain disproportionately clustered in traditionally female jobs with lower pay and fewer benefits." Furthermore, she points out, professional women earn less than their male counterparts: "In 1991 . . . women physicians earned 53.9 percent of the wages of male physicians, and women in sales occupations earned only 59.5 percent of the wages of men in equivalent positions." Affirmative action is still needed to counteract these continuing disparities, proponents insist.

Affirmative action for women is just one of the topics debated in the following chapter on antifemale discrimination in the workforce.

"Interactions at work subject women
to subtle and not-so-subtle
expressions of inequality—from
paternalism to sexual harassment,
from invisibility to ostracism."

WOMEN ARE VICTIMS OF DISCRIMINATION IN THE WORKPLACE

Barbara F. Reskin and Irene Padavic

In the following viewpoint, Barbara F. Reskin and Irene Padavic
argue that women face pervasive discrimination in the workplace. Such discrimination, the authors maintain, takes the form
of female segregation in lower-status, lower-wage positions, lack
of opportunities for advancement, and sexual harassment. Deep-
seated cultural stereotypes about women as well as male workers' desire to retain their privileged positions generate this antifemale discrimination in the workplace, the authors contend.
Reskin and Padavic are the authors of Women and Men at Work, from
which this viewpoint is excerpted.

As you read, consider the following questions:

1. What are the four kinds of sex inequality seen in the
   workplace, according to Reskin and Padavic?
2. What is paternalism, according to the authors?
3. According to Reskin and Padavic, how can customers'
   preferences create workplace discrimination?

The workplace is an important arena for sex inequality in our society. First, the workplace maintains sex differentiation by concentrating women and men in different settings and assigning them different duties. Second, sex differentiation in jobs leads to unequal earnings, authority, and social status for women and men, because jobs are the main way through which most adults acquire income and social standing. Finally, interactions at work subject women to subtle and not-so-subtle expressions of inequality—from paternalism to sexual harassment, from invisibility to ostracism.

Sex Inequality at Work

Sex inequality at work takes four forms:

• *Sex segregation.* Throughout history and around the world, societies have imposed a sexual division of labor in which women and men perform different tasks. . . . Like those in the rest of the world, America's workplaces are sex segregated. Fewer than 10 percent of Americans have a coworker of the other sex who does the same job, for the same employer, in the same location, and on the same shift. Of course other characteristics of workers besides their sex affect what jobs they get. Workplaces are segregated by race and ethnicity as well. African-American women are concentrated in different jobs than Mexican-American women, for example, who in turn are underrepresented in jobs in which European-American women predominate. The jobs in which women and men are segregated are not only different but also unequal.

• *Sex differences in promotions.* Women are concentrated at low levels in the organizations that employ them and in the lower ranks in their occupations and professions. Even in predominantly female lines of work, such as nursing, the higher the position, the more likely the job holder is to be male. Women are also more likely than men to work in dead-end jobs and, as a result, are less likely to be promoted. Even women who win jobs in middle management find top-level positions beyond their reach.

• *Sex differences in authority.* Employers tend to reserve powerful positions for men; women are less likely than men to exercise authority in the workplace. Women supervise fewer subordinates than men and are less likely to control financial resources. Even women managers—whose numbers have grown dramatically—are less likely than men to make decisions, especially decisions that are vital for their employer.

• *Sex differences in earnings.* Around the world, men outearn women. In 1992, for example, U.S. women who worked full time, year-round, earned just under 70 percent of what similar men earned. Put differently, for every dollar paid to a woman who worked full time, year-round, a man earned $1.43. What's more, men are more likely than women to have health insurance and other benefits. The consequences of this disparity in earnings and benefits follow workers into old age: Among retired persons, women's resources average about 60 percent of men's. . . .

How can we explain systematic sex inequality in the workplace? Social scientists have proposed a variety of explanations, including cultural beliefs, men's actions, [and] employers' actions. . . .

CULTURAL BELIEFS ABOUT GENDER AND WORK

A major category of explanations for sex inequality at work relates to culture. Indeed, gender is the paramount organizing principle in most societies. Societies go to great lengths to produce differences between the sexes in appearance, talents, hobbies, and so forth.

Clay Bennett, North America Syndicate. Reprinted by permission

Contemporary cultures are so riddled with sex stereotypes, or assumptions about individuals based on sex, that we all engage in stereotyped thinking. If a newscaster reports a complaint that a police officer used excessive force, most of us imagine a policeman wielding the nightstick. Some of us may not even think a policewoman is capable of such aggressiveness. In 1993 an elevator operator at the House of Representatives repeatedly told a newly elected African-American woman that she could not use an elevator reserved for members of the House. Finally it dawned on the elevator operator that the woman was a Representative. Note that cultural beliefs about men, women, and work affect everyone in a society: workers, customers, and clients, as well as the people who hire workers, assign them to jobs, and set their pay.

Unless someone directly challenges our assumptions about sex, race, and work, like the congressional elevator operator, we rarely question our stereotypes. This invisibility makes these assumptions especially powerful in shaping our behavior. If it never occurs to a branch manager that a female clerk might accept a promotion to night manager, he will not offer it to her. His assumptions about sex differences in workers' desire for promotion, need for a raise, willingness to work nights, or family responsibilities prevent him from considering whether he should offer the promotion to a woman. . . .

SEX STEREOTYPES

A poem by Alfred Lord Tennyson, although written in the mid 1800s, illustrates several contemporary sex stereotypes about work:

> Man for the field and women for the hearth:
> Man for the sword and for the needle she:
> Man with the head and woman with the heart:
> Man to command and woman to obey;
> All else confusion.

The first stereotype expressed in the poem is that women and men are naturally suited for different tasks. Second, the sexes supposedly differ innately, with men being governed by reason ("the head") and women by emotion ("the heart"). Third, men are assumed to be naturally suited to exercising authority over women. Finally, deviations from these natural patterns will allegedly lead to chaos.

Sex stereotypes like these, along with stereotypes about the characteristics that various jobs require, lead jobs to be labeled male or female. For example, Western culture stereotypes men as assertive and competitive. These notions, along with the assumptions that assertive salespeople sell more cars and that combative lawyers win more trials, imply that men will naturally outdo women at selling cars or arguing cases in court. Both sex stereotypes and job stereotypes are often off the mark. Insurance companies, for example, have learned that, although women can sell as aggressively as men, a soft sell is often more effective than a hard sell. Nonetheless, sex and job stereotypes contribute to various forms of sex inequality at work.

RELATIONSHIPS AND GENDER ROLES

Cultural beliefs about relationships between the sexes also contribute to sex inequality at work. The beliefs of fundamentalist Muslims, for example, which require the physical segregation of the sexes, give rise to employment patterns quite different from those in the Western world. In rural Muslim societies, this segregation has kept women out of the paid labor force and close to home, where they prepare food, do housework, deliver babies, and sew clothing.

Western and Eastern cultures share some beliefs that legitimate sex inequality. One of these is that men are inherently superior to women. This view supports greater job authority and higher pay for men.

A corollary of the ideology of male superiority is paternalism, the notion that women, like children, are inferior creatures whom men must take care of. The belief that men support women has helped to justify women's lower pay. The idea that women require protection has also helped exclude women from many jobs. Past actions of the battery manufacturer Johnson Controls illustrate how paternalism can reduce women's job options and pay. Johnson Controls barred women from all jobs that either exposed them to lead (which can cause birth defects) or led to jobs that could expose them to lead, unless they were surgically sterilized. In 1991 the Supreme Court ruled that Johnson's policy violated the Pregnancy Discrimination Act, but this decision was too late for the women who had already been sterilized or transferred to lower-paid work. . . .

PRESERVING ADVANTAGED POSITIONS

A different explanation for sex inequality rests on the idea that privileged or dominant groups try to preserve their advantaged position. Monarchs rarely give up their kingdoms, and millionaires are not known for ridding themselves of their fortunes; on the contrary, the rich and powerful are bent on retaining and even expanding their wealth and power. They do so in a variety of ways, from segregating subordinate groups to denying them the opportunity to acquire the skills needed to advance.

Men and women do not differ when it comes to the impulse to retain their advantages. Although women lack the power and the incentive to exclude men from "women's" jobs, history offers examples of white women resisting the entry of women of color into their domain. However, as a group, working men are indisputably better off than working women, even though many men—particularly men of color—hold low-paying, undesirable jobs, enjoy no authority at work, and have little chance of a promotion.

Why do men see women as threats to their advantaged position? Many men believe that women might take jobs away from men, outperform men in the same job, or lead employers to cut a job's pay. Furthermore, if women can perform "macho" jobs like coal mining, police work, or military combat, these jobs lose their capacity to confirm male workers' masculinity. Some men also fear that having female coworkers will lower the prestige of their work. A male law professor reportedly rejected a female applicant for a faculty position with this explanation: "This is a law school, not a god damn nursing school!" Finally, men may worry that women's equality at work will undermine men's privileges in other realms: If women earned as much as men and had as much authority at work, women could insist on greater equality in the family, the community, and national political life. In view of all the benefits that men, especially white men, enjoy because of their sex and race, it is not surprising that men sometimes take action to preserve their advantaged status.

EXCLUDING WOMEN

Like other groups concerned about competition from lower-paid workers, male workers' first line of defense has been to try to exclude women. One strategy is to prevent women from acquiring the necessary qualifications for customarily male jobs. Some unions, for example, have barred women from apprenticeship programs, and before 1970 professional schools admitted few women.

When entry barriers begin to give way and it is harder to exclude outsiders, some workers try to drive out newcomers by making them miserable on the job. For example, when the U.S. Department of the Treasury hired its first women in 1870, men blew smoke and spat tobacco juice at them and made catcalls. A hundred years later, women entering customarily male blue-collar jobs got similar treatment. An African-American woman who took a job as a sheet-metal worker recalled, "When I first starting working there, they gave me a hard time. . . . They would make wisecracks about what they would like to do. I just kept on walking . . . but it made me feel trampy." Another strategy to drive out female pioneers is to prevent their doing the job properly by denying them information, giving them the wrong tools, or sabotaging their work. Even if most men are neutral or welcoming, a few men can create a hostile environment.

EMPLOYERS' ACTIONS

It is employers who hire workers, assign them to jobs, decide whom to promote, and set pay. Most sex inequality at work results from these actions. Until recently, employers' main contribution to sex inequality was simply hiring few or no women for certain kinds of jobs. To understand how employers' hiring practices produce sex inequality, consider the three ways that employers locate most workers. Some employers choose from a pool of applicants, some use formal intermediaries such as employment agencies, and still others rely on referrals by employees. This third method—workers' referrals—is most common because it is free and effective (current workers screen out unacceptable job candidates). However, recruiting new employees through workers' referrals tends to perpetuate inequality. First, people's social networks tend to include others of the same sex, ethnicity, and race. Second, sex stereotypes, fears of competition, and concern with coworkers' and bosses' reactions prevent workers from recommending someone of the "wrong" sex or race. For example, a worker whose sister-in-law is looking for work may hesitate to nominate her for a job in his all-male department because his coworkers may be mad, his boss will hold him responsible if she doesn't measure up, and she may blame him if the boss or workers give her a hard time.

Employers also contribute to sex inequality through job assignments. Who ends up in what job is largely up to employers and managers, whose biases or stereotypes can lead them to assign women and men to different jobs. A lawsuit charging Lucky Stores, a West Coast grocery chain, with sex discrimination illustrates both the role of stereotypes and the impact of managerial discretion. At the trial, a Lucky's executive testified that his experience managing a store 30 years earlier had convinced him that "men preferred working on the floor to working at the cash register . . . and that women preferred working at the cash register." The qualifications that employers require also influence whom they assign to what jobs. Some organizations require qualifications that are more common among men and unnecessary to do the job. Requiring production experience or an MBA for a management job, for example, may unnecessarily restrict the number of women in the pool of job candidates.

Why might employers treat female and male workers differently? They may do so because of biases toward women or because they believe it will be more profitable in the long run.

Discrimination is treating people unequally because of personal characteristics that are not related to their performance. Few would claim that a local park is discriminating by refusing to hire a 9-year-old girl as lifeguard. Presumably, age is relevant to ensuring the safety of a pool full of swimmers (and the park wouldn't hire a 9-year-old boy either). In contrast, refusing to hire a 19-year-old because she is female is sex discrimination, because her sex is irrelevant to her ability to perform the job.

Around the world and for most of the history of the United States, employers have openly discriminated on the basis of sex, as well as on the basis of race, ethnicity, national origin, age, appearance, and sexual orientation. Employers have refused to hire women and other social minorities, segregated them into jobs different from those held by white men, denied them promotions, and paid them lower wages. Until quite recently, employers discriminated without a second thought. In the mid–nineteenth century, the publisher of the New York Herald, for example, stormed into the newspaper's office one day and bellowed, "Who are these females? Fire them all!" Although such discrimination seems outrageous today, until the early 1960s, it was both legal and commonplace. It took the civil rights movement of the early 1960s to persuade Americans that race discrimination is unfair and to spur Congress and state legislatures to outlaw employment discrimination based on sex and race.

Although antidiscrimination laws have prompted employers to change some of their practices, employers continue to discriminate illegally on the basis of people's sex, race, national origin, and age. (They also discriminate on the basis of people's appearance and sexual orientation, which is legal in most of the United States and the world.) In the last half of the 1980s, the Equal Employment Opportunities Commission received more than 30,000 complaints of sex discrimination per year, and nearly 80 percent of 803 Americans surveyed in 1990 believed that most if not all employers practice some form of job discrimination.

STATISTICAL DISCRIMINATION

Another reason for employers to discriminate against women is the fear that employing women will reduce profits because women are less productive or more costly to employ. The idea that women may be more expensive employees stems from the assumption that motherhood will cause women to miss more work than men or lead to higher turnover rates. The practice of treating individuals on the basis of beliefs about groups is called statistical discrimination. Although employers may legally refuse to hire or promote an individual who cannot do the job, it is illegal to treat an individual differently solely because she or he belongs to a group that is, on average, less productive or more costly to employ. Moreover, because employers are often wrong about which workers are productive, statistical discrimination is not necessarily good business.

Some employers treat men and women differently in deference to the prejudices of their customers or workers. Until the early 1970s, for example, airlines refused to hire male flight attendants because they claimed their passengers preferred stewardesses. Then the Supreme Court let stand a lower court ruling that customers' preferences do not justify sex discrimination, opening the occupation of flight attendant to men (and eventually to older people). Nonetheless, employers still defer to customers' preferences. For example, one lawsuit charged that a white male professor vetoed hiring a female to direct a Pacific-Asian studies program because he claimed that scholars and students from Japan would object to a female director.

Employers may also avoid hiring women out of fear that male workers will take offense. Male workers might sabotage the women's productivity, insist on higher pay to work with women, or even go on strike. . . .

IN SUM

Sex inequality in the workplace is manifested in several ways: The sexes are concentrated in different occupations; women are often confined to lower-ranking positions than men and are less likely than men to exercise authority; women earn less than men. Social scientists have advanced several explanations for these disparities: cultural factors, sex stereotypes, the preservation of male advantage, and discrimination by employers.

| "Women's current economic position relative to men is more a product of individual choices than of third-party discrimination."

WOMEN ARE NOT VICTIMS OF DISCRIMINATION IN THE WORKPLACE

Michael Lynch and Katherine Post

Working women do not face significant job discrimination, argue Michael Lynch and Katherine Post in the following viewpoint. Many women earn less than men because they choose careers that pay less than careers typically chosen by men, the authors contend. In addition, they maintain, most women work less hours than men work and therefore cannot achieve job seniority as quickly as men do. Lynch and Post assert, moreover, that women who do achieve seniority earn as much as or more than their male counterparts. Lynch is the Washington bureau chief for *Reason*, a monthly libertarian magazine. Post is a public policy fellow in the Washington office of the Pacific Research Institute.

As you read, consider the following questions:

1. Why is the "wage gap" an inaccurate indicator of discrimination, according to Lynch and Post?
2. According to the authors, why do women tend to be clustered into certain occupations?
3. What were the findings of the February 1996 *Working Women* survey, according to the authors?

From Michael Lynch and Katherine Post, "What Glass Ceiling?" Reprinted with permission of the authors and the *Public Interest*, no. 124, Summer 1996, pp. 27-36; ©1996 by National Affairs, Inc.

As the debate over affirmative action heats up, a concerted effort will be made to convince women that they are victims of job discrimination. A constitutional initiative in California . . . threatens to abolish public-sector preference programs, and, indeed, opponents of the initiative are appealing to women to oppose it. The National Organization for Women (NOW), for example, has made defeating the California Civil Rights Initiative (CCRI) its number one priority for 1996, and such formerly non-political groups as the YWCA have joined the charge to defeat it. [The CCRI won in November 1996.]

We completed a study in which we reviewed existing studies in this area; we have also compiled relevant data from the Census Bureau and the Bureau of Labor Statistics. Our findings, which are consistent with those of other scholars, are: (1) the wage gap has been closing in recent years, and that, when the data are controlled for relevant variables, it virtually disappears; and (2) the so-called glass ceiling is more a product of relative ages and qualifications of men and women than of explicit discrimination. In general, we found that women's current economic position relative to men is more a product of individual choices than of third-party discrimination.

IS THERE REALLY A WAGE GAP?

In the 1960s, feminist activists donned "59 cents" buttons to decry the fact that women, on average, earned 59 cents for every dollar a man earned. They maintained that this was hard proof of "gender" discrimination. By 1995, however, women were earning 74 cents for every dollar earned by a man; but preference advocates still called for government involvement in the economy to redress gender discrimination.

The wage-gap figure has proved to be a powerful political tool, though it is less useful as a measure of discrimination. As a statistical aggregate, the wage gap is only an amalgamation of all of the wages paid to women divided by all of the wages paid to men. To infer discrimination from such an aggregate, one must assume that the factors that determine wages—such as education level and concentration, field of work, and continuous time in the workforce—are constant across the sexes. As it happens, such an assumption is highly suspect. In fact, even when a particular wage-gap figure is advertised as having been corrected for such factors, this is usually only partially true.

For example, it is true that women earn less than men at every level of education achieved. In 1994, among those who held bachelor's degrees, women earned 76 cents on the male dollar.

This ratio increased to 79 cents for those with master's degrees and to 85 cents for those with doctorates. The implication that is usually drawn is that, since the data is controlled for education, the remaining disparity proves that women continue to face discrimination in compensation levels. This level of aggregation, however, fails to account both for the fields in which men and women hold degrees and for the actual fields in which the graduates find employment. Residual differences in earnings are best explained by variations in choices of educational and career fields, not discrimination.

MEN AND WOMEN CHOOSE DIFFERENT CAREERS

In 1992, more than one-third of the bachelor's degrees earned by women were in communications, education, English literature, the health professions, and the visual and performing arts. Of the bachelor's degrees earned by men in 1992, only 17 percent were in these fields. In the same year, 26 percent of men who earned bachelor's degrees did so in business, compared to 20 percent of women. Thirteen percent of men's bachelor's degrees were earned in engineering, compared to 2 percent of women's.

The contrast becomes more striking when we move from bachelor's to advanced degrees (master's and doctorates). While one out of four women who earned Ph.D.s did so in education—a field in which an individual with an advanced degree earns, on average, a mean monthly income of $3,048—one out of five men who earned doctorates did so in engineering, a field in which an individual with an advanced degree, on average, earns a mean monthly income of $4,049.

In 1992 . . . women earned 75 percent of the advanced degrees conferred in education, 70 percent of the advanced degrees conferred in public administration, 65 percent of the advanced degrees conferred in English literature, and 63 percent of the advanced degrees conferred in ethnic and cultural studies. In this same year, by contrast, men earned 86 percent of the advanced degrees conferred in engineering, 75 percent of the advanced degrees conferred in physical sciences and science technologies, 65 percent of the advance degrees conferred in business management and administrative services, and 60 percent of advanced degrees conferred in mathematics.

Furthermore, it must be emphasized that these figures are for one year and do not represent the total labor pool. The wage-gap figures, however, are based on the total pool. Since women have increased their representation in such fields as business and engineering in recent years, these 1992 figures overstate the proportion of women qualified to work in these fields.

Thus if we examine cumulative figures, we find even more pronounced differences. As of 1990, more than one in four women who held a bachelor's degree or higher earned that degree in education, while less than one in ten men who held a bachelor's degree or higher earned that degree in education. By this same year, nearly one in four men who held a bachelor's degree or higher earned that degree in business management and nearly one in six men held a degree in engineering. By contrast, less than one in eight women who held a degree in 1990 earned that degree in business management and less than 2 in 100 in engineering. As to be expected, these different concentrations hold major implications for earnings. Regardless of the sex of its holder, the market demand dictates that a degree in engineering is worth more than a degree in education.

JOB DISCRIMINATION OR PERSONAL CHOICE?

Many feminists interpret the above data as precisely the problem: Women's work is undervalued relative to men's. The truth is that all professions have costs and benefits that are both monetary and non-monetary. While investment bankers make more money than school teachers, teachers derive non-monetary benefits—e.g., long summer breaks—which are not available on Wall Street. It must also be noted that it is entirely consistent with economic theory for wages to drop in an industry in which a significant number of women enter. If women suddenly enter a field previously dominated by men, and if there is not a reduction in male participation in the field, overall labor supply will increase, thus exerting downward pressure on wages.

There are also psychological reasons why women have historically tended to concentrate in certain fields. For example, the preponderance of evidence suggests that women, on average, have a stronger preference for children than do men. It is this difference, concludes Stanford economist Victor R. Fuchs, which contributes to women's economic disadvantage. While this claim continues to be debated, a myriad of both statistical and anecdotal evidence supports it. In 1995, the Whirlpool Foundation, in conjunction with the Families and Work Institute, sponsored a poll conducted by Louis Harris and Associates, Inc. The results were published as a study entitled "Women: The New Providers." Some of this study's findings indicate that women, more so than men, define success in terms of home and family. "The New Providers" found that "family remains at the core of what's important for women, whether they work inside or outside the home." Only 15 percent of the women polled would work full time if they didn't feel they had to financially, while more than twice that of men would.

Expectations about the future also shape the fields women enter. June O'Neill, the current director of the Congressional Budget Office, has pointed out that, as recently as the late 1960s, less than 30 percent of the women in the National Longitudinal Survey of Youth expected to be working at age 35, even though more than 70 percent actually were. As a result, it made little sense for women of this generation to spend time and resources acquiring skills that they didn't expect to use. Moreover, it made sense for those women, who expected to spend time outside of the workforce raising a family, to specialize in flexible fields, such as teaching. Thus rational self-interest, not discrimination, appears to account for women's occupational clustering.

FEWER HOURS MEAN LESS PAY

In addition to the fact that men and women vary in the fields in which they specialize, they also differ in the amount of time they devote to paid work. The accumulated evidence shows that, even as the gap between labor-force participation rates of men and women closes, men consistently work more hours than women.

A 1992 Census study on the relationship between education level and earnings found that, at every level of education, men have more months with work activity than women. A 1984 Census study found that, while only 1.6 percent of a man's work years were spent away from work, 14.7 percent of a woman's work years were spent away from work—an eightfold difference. This prompted the U.S. Department of Labor (DOL) to conclude that "women spend significantly more time away from work and are apparently unable to build the seniority that men achieve." In addition, the DOL noted that the turnover rates are higher for women than for men.

With less seniority, it is hardly surprising that women's earnings are, on average, lower than men's. A 1990 National Bureau of Economic Research working paper found "a very strong connection between job seniority and wages in the typical employment relationship: other things held constant, 10 years of job seniority raises the wage of the typical worker by over 25 percent." In addition, women who work still put in less time than men. DOL data show that, in 1994, 55 percent of women worked 40 or more hours a week compared to 75 percent of men. While 16 percent of men worked 55 or more hours a week that same year, only 6 percent of women did. Again, it is reasonable to expect that someone who works 55 hour weeks will earn more, over time, than someone who works 40 hours, regardless of whether they are male or female. While it is simply common sense to conclude that those who work more produce more and, as a result, earn more, these inconvenient facts are often ignored.

A DISAPPEARING WAGE GAP

The pay gap between men and women virtually disappears when age, educational attainment, and continuous time spent in the workforce are factored in as wage determinants. In fact, this is neither a new phenomenon nor a product of preference programs. Economist Thomas Sowell has shown that, as early as 1971, never-married women in their thirties who had worked continuously earned slightly higher incomes than men of the same description. In the academic world, single women who earned Ph.D.s in the 1930s became full professors by the 1950s at slightly higher rates than their male counterparts. In addition, never-married academic women earned slightly more money in some years than men of the same description.

Similarly, June O'Neill has found that women between the ages of 27 and 33 who had never had a child earned nearly 98 percent as much as men in this same demographic. In another study, O'Neill and Solomon Polachek found that the gap in earnings between men and women with Ph.D.s in economics was a mere 5 percent.

THE TRUTH ABOUT THE "WAGE GAP"

The so-called "wage gap," which by 1995 amounted to 74 cents for women, compared with one dollar for men, is calculated by adding all of the wages paid to women divided by all of the wages paid to men. It does not account for the many varied factors that contribute to wages, like seniority, education, continuous time in the work force, and the choices individuals make about their careers.

Mona Charen, *Conservative Chronicle*, September 4, 1996.

A less scientific but more comprehensive salary survey by *Working Woman* magazine in February 1996 indicates a shrinking wage gap as well. Compiling data on 250 positions in 38 industries, the *Working Woman* survey found that, on average, women in the study earned 85 percent to 95 percent of what men in similar positions earned. While there were some fields in which women earned much less than men, there were other fields, such as university administrators, in which they earned more. In fact, while pay for males has dropped 11 percent since 1974, the average female worker's pay has increased by 6.1 percent. For women in high-powered jobs, pay levels have shot up 16.4 percent. This is consistent with data from a 1992 study by Korn/Ferry International, which found that women had reached the base salary of $100,000 at a younger age than the men polled in their 1989 survey. More than 50 percent of women were already earning $100,000 by the time they reached 40, while at that age, only 31 percent of men were earning at least $100,000. . . .

THE NEWS IS GOOD

The advocates of sex-based preferences argue in part that affirmative action is necessary to overcome discrimination and to ensure the economic progress that women are due. In fact, as we have shown, women have made a great deal of economic progress over the last several decades, to the point that qualified women who do the same work as similarly qualified men receive the same pay as men (and sometimes more). The differences that now exist are the result of individual choices, not of third-party discrimination. That is good news, and it is a shame that it will be obscured by the political head-counting that will undoubtedly occur in the debates that lie ahead.

"Only 3–5 percent of senior
positions are held by women—far
too few in proportion to their
numbers in the labor force."

WORKING WOMEN FACE BARRIERS
TO ADVANCEMENT

Federal Glass Ceiling Commission

The Federal Glass Ceiling Commission was formed in 1991 to
foster advancement of women and minorities to high-level decisionmaking positions in business. In the following viewpoint,
excerpted from a 1995 report, the commission maintains that
women have made some progress in advancing to upper-level
management positions but continue to face obstacles to promotion. According to the commission, these obstacles include gender stereotyping, sexual harassment, exclusion from mentoring
and crucial work assignments, and placement in dead-end positions traditionally reserved for women. The authors argue that
these impediments create an invisible barrier—often referred to
as the workplace's "glass ceiling"—that keeps many women
from attaining senior-level positions.

As you read, consider the following questions:

1. How many Fortune 1000 companies have female chief
   executive officers (CEOs), according to the commission?
2. According to the authors, how do most male CEOs respond
   to questions about the existence of a glass ceiling?
3. How do female executives' earnings compare with male
   executives' earnings, according to the commission?

Excerpted from *Good for Business: Making Full Use of the Nation's Human Capital: The Environmental
Scan*, a fact-finding report of the Federal Glass Ceiling Commission, Washington, D.C.,
March 1995.

A classic glass ceiling for women still exists, despite the fact that over the past decade women have moved slowly up the ladder in the largest U.S. corporations. Still, only 3–5 percent of senior positions are held by women—far too few in proportion to their numbers in the labor force. . . . Many of the 439 female senior executives who participated in a 1992 Korn/Ferry International Survey are not convinced that the battle is won, [but] their views of the future are generally optimistic.

FEMALE EXECUTIVES' PROGRESS

The Fortune companies' influence in the marketplace is substantial. They often serve as bellwethers of change. It is significant, therefore, that two Fortune 1000 companies are now headed by white female CEOs. Furthermore, the presence and visibility of women executives have influenced the appointment of women to corporate boards of directors. For the Fortune 1000 companies, the number of directorships (board seats) held by women increased 13 percent from 1993 to 1994 (731 to 814). The number of women serving on boards increased by 14 percent from 1993 to 1994 (500 to 570). According to a 1994 Catalyst survey women occupied only 6.9 percent of the seats on corporate boards of directors—up from 6.2 percent in 1993. Half of the Fortune 500 Industrial Service companies have at least one female board member. Approximately half of the 70 new women on boards have never before served on a Fortune 500/Service 500 board. Sixty-four companies that had no women on their boards in 1993 now have at least one female director. Each of the ten most profitable Fortune 500 companies has at least one female director and five have two.

A 1992 Heidrick & Struggles report, *Minorities and Women on Corporate Boards,* based on a survey of 806 public Fortune companies, showed that white women held 5.3 percent of board seats, African American women, 0.3 percent, Hispanic American women, 0.1 percent, and Asian and Pacific Islander American women, 0.01 percent. (White men held 88.9 percent of the board seats, African American men, 1.8 percent, Hispanic American men, 0.7 percent, and Asian and Pacific Islander American men, 0.2 percent. . . .)

CEO SURVEY RESULTS

Contrary to indications from current data, the majority of the CEO participants in the Federal Glass Ceiling Commission's survey believe that women no longer confront serious glass ceiling problems. [The Commission surveyed twenty-five CEOs from white- and minority-owned businesses regarding their perceptions and experiences in recruiting and promoting women.] The CEOs were encouraged by the fact that the successful performance of women in top-level positions was overcoming the stereotypes that have historically limited women's upward mobility. The CEOs did admit that the attitudes and biases of middle-level managers continue to create barriers to the advancement of women. Catalyst research also shows that acceptance of traditional stereotypes of women has influenced middle managers to move women to staff rather than to the line jobs that relate directly to a company's profitability and lead to the positions above the glass ceiling.

On the other hand, a 1990 Financial Women International survey of male CEOs and female vice presidents indicated a distinct disparity between the men's and women's perceptions of the existence of a glass ceiling. Seventy-three percent of the male CEOs said they don't think there is a glass ceiling; seventy-one percent of the female vice presidents think there is. Polly DiGiovacchino, president of the group that conducted the survey, pointed out, "There is definitely a gap between reality and perception."

The CEOs who were interviewed did not differentiate between minority and white women except to state that they believed that compensation parity between white non-Hispanic women and other women of color had been achieved. Data, however, show that very few Hispanic women and women of color are employed in private sector management and very few have advanced into senior positions. . . .

HOW CEOS PERCEIVE THE GLASS CEILING

The majority of the CEOs interviewed in the Glass Ceiling Commission survey think of the glass ceiling as something that used to affect women—white and non-white—but that is no longer a real problem for them. Without exception they expressed strong support for the concept of women's advancement to corporate senior management.

Although most CEOs thought that compensation parity between white non-Hispanic women and minority women had been reached, they agreed that parity between women and white non-Hispanic men had not been achieved, either in terms of equal access to senior decisionmaking jobs or in compensation. However, the majority of CEOs interviewed demonstrated that their companies had some women above the glass ceiling or ready to move through it. The majority of these companies had other women managers steadily climbing the promotion ladder. . . .

LITTLE OPPORTUNITY TO ADVANCE

In 1994, the Women's Bureau fielded both a popular and a scientific sample on what it means to be working women in America today. The Working-Women-Count! Survey reflects a consensus among working women about what's wrong with their jobs and what needs to be fixed—a consensus that crosses all occupations and incomes, all generations and races and all regions of the country. When asked to evaluate their current job, respondents gave "ability to advance" the highest negative ratings. Almost half the sample (46.6 percent) said they have little or no opportunity to advance, and an additional 14.2 percent say that advancement does not apply to them in their job situations, bringing the total who believe they cannot advance to 60.8 percent. These responses, as well as the findings of other surveys, suggest that we barely are scratching the surface of the glass.

Ida L. Castro, Insight, February 10, 1997.

Although some CEOs admitted that it is not always easy to persuade managers down the line to change their attitudes and practices that have limited the mobility of women and minorities, the CEOs interviewed are generally sanguine about the glass ceiling. They believe either that it no longer applies to women or that it is about to disappear for women. They recognize that the number of women at the top is still small, but they believe that change is inevitable.

Remarks made by CEOs on the topic of women and the glass ceiling include:

- "Gender is not a problem in finding highly qualified employees."
- "The issue has to be forced but if the minorities and women are hired on merit and can compete, there is grudging acceptance. The first time we hired a woman she went through a zillion interviews and there was deep resistance. Now we

hire men and women at a 60/40 ratio, and we'd be comfortable with 50/50. The men have seen that the women are high performers. Now there are women who outrank men and who supervise men with no problem."

- "I question the pernicious, sexist, and racist assumptions of the phrases 'qualified women' and 'qualified minorities.' We don't find it necessary to talk about qualified males."

HOW WHITE WOMEN PERCEIVE GLASS CEILING ISSUES

The perceptions quoted in this section are drawn from the testimony of women who spoke at the five public hearings sponsored by the Glass Ceiling Commission, from a 1992 Catalyst study, *Women in Engineering: An Untapped Resource*, and from Jane White's book, *A Few Good Women: Breaking the Barriers to Top Management*.

- "As an upper-level manager and an executive for [a major hotel chain] I kind of feel like I'm on the other side sometimes. I will say though that, contrary to some of my male counterparts who wonder what is the glass ceiling, they don't understand the terms. They don't see it, so they're not sure that it's even there."
- "It was amazing to me that in that short time period, an employer would take up valuable minutes asking about family instead of qualifications for the job. I myself was asked how many words I typed per minute. . . I guess I was fool enough to think that graduating magna cum laude from undergraduate and completing my juris doctor degree would alleviate the emphasis on my typing abilities."
- "It's not whether you're effective in getting results, it's a question of whether you fit some view of what a wife or mistress or daughter or somebody ought to look like."
- "People build their expectations on the basis of experience, and they come to these environments where there are nine men and one woman, and they immediately think that I am the one who brings papers or takes coats."
- "My boss is somewhat uncomfortable with me because I am a woman at a high level. He has told me so.". . .

MYTHS VS. FACTS

The findings of a 1992 Korn/Ferry survey of women in senior management positions in the Fortune 1000 industrial and 500 service companies refute many of the popular stereotypes about women that have been cited for why "they are not senior management material." For example:

- Women are not as committed to their careers as men, yet

only a third of the women had ever taken a leave of absence. Almost two-thirds of these leaves were for less than six months and 82 percent of these leaves were for maternity or other family reasons. *If maternity is controlled for, more men in the Korn/Ferry surveys took leaves of absence than did women.*

- Women will not work long hours, yet the respondents in the Korn/Ferry survey worked an average of 56 hours a week in 1992. This is the same number of hours reported by their male counterparts in a similar 1989 Korn/Ferry survey.
- Women cannot or will not relocate, yet only 14.1 percent of the women in the 1992 survey refused relocation. Twenty percent of their male counterparts reported refusing relocation in the 1989 Korn/Ferry survey. It is interesting to note that Korn/Ferry found that women *are not asked to relocate* as frequently as men. The failure to provide this opportunity may prejudice their chances for advancement.
- Women lack quantitative skills, yet 23 percent of women and 27 percent of men have spent most of their corporate careers in finance. Sixteen percent of men and 26 percent of women are in the commercial banking or diversified financial sectors.
- Women are warmer and more nurturing than men, yet *"concern for people"* was cited as important by 33 percent of men and only 18 percent of women in the Korn/Ferry surveys. . . .

HOW ARE FEMALE MANAGERS FARING?

Commission research and review of nongovernment surveys reveal the following information and data on where women are in Corporate America and how they are faring:

• The representation of women in the private sector differs significantly by group. According to the 1991 Earnings and Employment Surveys of the Bureau of Labor Statistics, U.S. Department of Labor, the following percentages of women managers were in the private sector:

- 35 percent of all white non-Hispanic women managers were in the private sector
- 3.4 percent of all African American women managers were in the private sector
- 2.0 percent of all Hispanic American women managers were in the private sector
- 1.2 percent of all Asian and Pacific Islander American women managers were in the private sector, and
- 0.2 percent of all American Indian women managers were in the private sector.

• Research reveals that women of all racial/ethnic groups are more likely to be employed in the service industries and in finance, insurance, real estate, and the wholesale/retail trade industries than are men. Nearly 75 percent of employed women work in these industries.

• Some Catalyst research suggests that male managers in these industries are reluctant to risk placing women in line positions because of stereotypes and preconceptions about women these managers hold.

• Given this reluctance, it is not surprising that a Catalyst survey found that women in the private sector are still concentrated in staff positions in "traditionally" female functional areas such as human resources, corporate communications, community and government relations, and the staff side of marketing and finance.

BARRIERS TO ADVANCEMENT

• Minority women experience the same barriers as white non-Hispanic women but the impact on them is greater. Because their numbers are smaller there are fewer male or female role models of the same race or ethnicity, and they are subject to racial and ethnic stereotypes as well as general stereotypes about women.

• Opportunities for advancement by minorities and women to senior positions, and especially for minority women, are limited by job placement that influences pay and advancement. The Commission's research papers suggest that women are often steered into jobs that limit possibilities for their career growth. Examples include gender- and race-based stereotyping of jobs, pay inequities, and "mommy-track" policies.

• The lack of family-friendly workplace practices is often cited as a barrier for female managers who must juggle home and professional responsibilities. Commission research shows that when companies do offer such programs, only a few career managers—male or female—take advantage of them, largely because they perceive that it may prejudice a climb up the corporate ladder. But glass ceiling research also reveals that those women who have availed themselves of the benefits of family-friendly programs have not sacrificed their opportunity for advancement.

SOME ENCOURAGING CHANGES

• Despite the obstacles women have faced in getting on the track to senior management they have persisted, persevered, and delivered high performance. As a consequence, an increasing number who have been in Corporate America for a dozen or more years are playing senior leadership roles and 60 percent of the female executives surveyed in the 1992 Korn/Ferry report that they expect to be members of the top senior management team by the year 2000. (This is an increase over the proportion of women in the 1982 Korn/Ferry survey who expected to break through to the top.)

• The experience of the Korn/Ferry survey participants reveals that the following additional encouraging changes have occurred over the decade:

  • Between 1982 and 1992, the proportion of women holding the title of Executive Vice President rose from 4 percent to 9 percent.

  • In that same period, the proportion of women at the senior vice president level rose from 13 percent to 23 percent.

• Commission research shows that women appear to have the best opportunity for advancement into management and decisionmaking positions in three types of industries:

  • Those which are fast-growing, for example, business services.

  • Those where change (i.e., deregulation or restructuring) has occurred, for example, in telecommunications.

  • Those with a female-intensive workforce, for example, insurance and banking.

Women's advances in title and responsibility are also being reflected in rising levels of compensation. For example:

  • Korn/Ferry surveys in 1982 and 1992 show that in those 10 years *average annual base salary plus bonus* for senior women executives rose from $92,000 to $187,00

  • The same surveys show that 30 percent of senior women executives earned over $200,000 in 1992 versus only 2.7 percent in 1982.

SLOW PROGRESS

The progress made by women senior executives does not mean that their earnings are comparable to male executives. The predominantly male sample of the 1989 Korn/Ferry survey showed an *average annual base salary plus bonus* of $289,000. (Part of the $102,000 difference in average compensation between the men surveyed in 1989 and the women surveyed in 1992 may be due to the shorter average tenures of the women. A significant number of women may just be entering their higher earning years.)

White women are advancing but progress is slow. Minority women are even more severely underrepresented in senior management in the private sector than their white female peers. Nonetheless, growing numbers of women—minority and non-minority—are earning the credentials required for senior management positions.

Public hearings, glass ceiling research, and private studies all indicate that the major barriers to the achievement of senior management positions by women in the private sector are these:

- Clustering of women in "traditionally female positions" that are dead-end
- Resistance of many middle-level and upper-level managers to place women in the line positions that feed into the senior management positions above the glass ceiling
- Lack of mentoring and lack of access to assignments and job rotation that provide visibility
- Exclusion from informal communications networks
- Prevalence of bias, insensitivity, and incidents of sexual harassment
- Lower compensation levels which act to disqualify high-potential women as executive search firm candidates when corporations are looking outside for senior managers.

| "Women now have equality of opportunity and . . . those who choose to rise to high positions in corporations can do so."

WORKING WOMEN DO NOT FACE BARRIERS TO ADVANCEMENT

Diana Furchtgott-Roth

In the following viewpoint, Diana Furchtgott-Roth argues that working women who desire job promotions are not limited by a "glass ceiling"—the term commonly used to describe discriminatory barriers to career advancement for women. According to the author, the glass ceiling is a myth promoted by feminists in an attempt to gain unfair preferential treatment for female workers. She contends that women have actually made significant progress in attaining high-level positions and that whatever pay and promotion disparities exist between male and female workers are the result not of discrimination but of women's personal career choices. Furchtgott-Roth is a resident fellow at the American Enterprise Institute, a conservative think tank. She is also coauthor of *Women's Figures: The Economic Progress of Women in America*.

As you read, consider the following questions:

1. According to the author, why is the contention that only 5 percent of senior managers at Fortune 2000 companies are women inaccurate?
2. Why do many working mothers choose not to pursue high-level executive positions, according to Furchtgott-Roth?
3. In the author's opinion, how might the "glass-ceiling myth" backfire?

It has become fashionable to talk about a glass ceiling for women, an invisible career barrier which cannot be overcome by hardworking females with even the most impeccable qualifications. Its a sad story of women who work shoulder to shoulder with men and then, just as that chief executive officer job comes into view . . . presto!, the glass barrier descends. The men move up; the women are left behind.

The glass ceiling was given the seal of credibility with the federal Glass Ceiling Commission in 1991, which put out a ponderous report authenticating these claims. And other institutions, most recently the New York firm Catalyst, periodically release studies showing that women make up only a small fraction of corporate officers at the nation's largest companies. The conclusion of all these studies, of course, is that life is unfair to women, who need special affirmative-action programs to progress in the workplace.

But is this sad story true, or is it just the fantasy of a group of whiny females for whom the tale of the glass ceiling is a convenient way of advancing their own interests? In fact, the glass ceiling is a figment of feminist imaginations, up there with the myths of alar poisoning, and Jews eating Christian babies on Passover.

FEMINISTS' AND DIVERSITY SPECIALISTS' INTERESTS

Why was this tale concocted? The answer is obvious: It's in the interests of feminists to portray women as victims, since it gives women greater economic benefits. Who wouldn't want preferred access to government contracts, promotion of less-qualified members of their group over others and a whole apparatus set up to ensure proper representation of their relevant group? As a woman professional, I should be delighted, except that it imposes substantial economic costs on society as a whole, shared by all consumers and taxpayers.

Efforts in corporations, universities and governments to counteract the so-called glass ceiling in the name of equality rely on a whole cadre of "diversity specialists" whose role is to ensure equal representation of various groups in different professions. Corporations hold sensitivity training rather than computer training and promote the less-qualified to managerial positions to be "fair." Universities have quotas for female faculty and governments have minority set-asides.

All of this costs money, reduces efficiency and results in higher prices for corporations' products, higher tuition costs at universities and higher taxes for individuals. Economic growth is slowed, reducing job creation—the most important avenue for everyone's advancement. Yes, some women win—but everyone else pays for it.

Women Have Made Much Progress

Just consider some facts: Today women are well-represented in the professions; they continue to enter fields of study previously dominated by men; they are starting their own businesses in record numbers; and they are winning elective office throughout the country. Laws barring discrimination against women are on the books and enforced. All those gains clearly contradict the image of women as victims struggling against discrimination in the workplace.

Since 1982 women have earned more than 50 percent of all bachelors degrees and all masters degrees, and in other fields women are closing the gap fast. Whereas 2 or 3 percent of all law degrees awarded went to women in the fifties and sixties and 5 percent in 1970, women now earn about 43 percent of those degrees. Fewer than 1 percent of dentistry degrees were awarded to women in the fifties, sixties and seventies, yet women now receive 38 percent of these degrees. Similar trends hold for doctoral and medical degrees. In 1996 women represented 54 percent of the class admitted to Yale Medical School.

What Glass Ceiling?

The Federal Glass Ceiling Commission—75 percent female in composition—complains in its report that women can't get anywhere because of "white male prejudices." The credibility of the allegation is impaired not only by female domination of the Commission, but also by their career successes: a U.S. senator, two U.S. Representatives, a bank president, corporate vice presidents and senior vice presidents, attorneys, and presidents of consulting firms. Ambition has taken on new meaning if these women consider themselves held down by "the Glass Ceiling."

Paul Craig Roberts, *Washington Times*, March 24, 1995.

As they move into previously male-dominated fields, women's wages have been steadily rising relative to men's wages. It is true that, on average, women earn less than men, when all women's wages are averaged with all men's wages. But that is because these averages compare people who have different educational backgrounds and who have chosen different jobs and different hours. When comparing wages, like should be compared to like, not nurses to engineers.

In studies accounting for demographic and job characteristics such as education, race, age, part- or full-time employment, public- or private-sector status, occupation and union or non-union status, women earn almost as much as men. The National Longitudinal Survey of Youth found that, among people ages 27 to 33 who never have had a child, women's earnings are close to 98 percent of men's. A study of economics and engineering doctorates by June O'Neill came up with similar results. However, many women choose occupations and careers that allow them more flexibility in work hours, and these positions typically pay less.

Furthermore, the wage gap widens once women have children, presumably since the children place additional demands on these women's time.

The most outstanding gains made by women lately have been in the business world. In 1972 there were only 400,000 women-owned businesses. Today there are approximately 8 million such businesses in the United States, employing 15.5 million people and generating $1.4 trillion in sales. The number of women-owned businesses increased 43 percent from 1987 to 1992. Women are starting businesses at twice the rate of men.

INACCURATE DATA ON WOMEN'S PROGRESS

With all this progress, why did the Glass Ceiling Commission conclude that only 5 percent of senior managers at Fortune 2000 companies are women, leading to charges of glass ceilings and discrimination? Because the commission used a statistically corrupt methodology to prove its point and further its agenda. Rather than comparing the number of women qualified to hold top positions with those who actually hold those jobs, it compared the number of women in the labor force, without reference to experience or education levels, with those wielding power at top corporations. This resulted in a politically useful low number of 5 percent.

The real answer is that there are comparatively few educated and experienced women available to be nominated for such high-level positions. Typical qualifications for top management positions include both a masters degree in business administration and 25 years of work experience, and there aren't many such women around. Look at the data: Women received less than 5 percent of graduate degrees in the sixties and seventies, and these are the graduates who now are at the pinnacle of their professions. That supports the "pipeline" theory, which holds that women have not reached the top in greater numbers because they have not been "in the pipeline" long enough.

Moreover, to reach the CEO level, individuals have to be committed to their jobs and work 60-hour weeks continuously throughout their career. Many men and many women, especially mothers, do not want to do this. Moving in and out of the workforce in accordance with family demands is not conducive to being a CEO of a major corporation. Yet many mothers do interrupt their careers in just this fashion, since these mothers believe that they are the best caregivers for their children.

WOMEN ARE NOT GLASS-CEILING VICTIMS

There is nothing wrong with choosing a career which allows more time at home with less pay rather than one with more time at work with more pay, and in either case women should not be considered victims of a glass ceiling and in need of government intervention such as affirmative action. One consequence of those choices, however, is that out of the relatively small group of women who have the educational requirements and training to be CEOs—those who got their graduate degrees in the sixties—fewer have put in the 25 years of 60-hour weeks that a CEO position requires. The result is a small pool of qualified women for those kinds of positions.

The good news is that in the future more women will be getting the necessary educational qualifications and more of those who graduated in the seventies and later will be moving into corporate positions, so the trend toward increasing numbers of female corporate executives will continue. However, because of the unique position that mothers play in rearing children, the ratio of male to female CEOs is unlikely to reach 50-50. This is not necessarily bad. The important point is that women should be free to choose their career paths.

Now, if outcomes at the CEO level are not likely to be 50-50 on their own, does that show that women face a glass ceiling? Not at all: The data make it clear that women now have equality of opportunity and that those who choose to rise to high positions in corporations can do so. Cultural barriers to women in top positions largely have disappeared—just ask Secretary of State Madeleine Albright. When discrimination does occur, there are legal remedies to deal with it under the Civil Rights Act and the Equal Pay Act. Women are bringing these cases to court and winning.

Whereas the glass-ceiling myth benefits women in the short run, its effects well could backfire against women over the long term. With special preferences for women in the workplace, the achievements of all women can be called into question, since it can be assumed that progress has been made because of quotas and preferences rather than ability. When Albright's selection was announced, there was some speculation that President Clinton had chosen her because of her sex rather than because of her preeminent qualifications. Albright was confirmed by the Senate irrespective of these doubts. But the patients shopping for heart surgeons or the retirees looking for financial planners well may prefer to put their lives and their money into male hands, even though the particular female heart surgeons and financial planners under consideration may not have benefited from affirmative action.

Some say that women in America face a glass ceiling: that they are paid less than men; that they cannot reach the highest rungs of the corporate ladder; that they cannot enter any profession they choose; that they would benefit from more government intervention in the marketplace; and that they need affirmative action and quotas. But none of these is true. These views are being advanced because it is in feminists' interests for women to have preferential treatment and to have all consumers and taxpayers pay for it. It's a great scam—and they're getting away with it.

| "Women executives who take time off and later go back to work permanently sacrifice career advancement and earning potential."

WORKING MOTHERS ARE DISCRIMINATED AGAINST

Deborah L. Jacobs

Women who take time off from their careers to raise children often find limited opportunities when they return to work, asserts Deborah L. Jacobs in the following viewpoint. In comparison to other employees, Jacobs contends, mothers returning to work usually discover that they will have smaller salaries, less respect from co-workers, lower job prestige, and fewer opportunities for advancement. Jacobs, an independent journalist based in New York, specializes in legal and business topics.

As you read, consider the following questions:
1. According to Jacobs, why could businesses be suffering a "brain drain" of women professionals?
2. What percentage of American workers are women, according to the author?
3. What did Professor Joy Schneer discover about the salaries of women who took time off from work to raise children, according to Jacobs?

From Deborah L. Jacobs, "Back from the Mommy Track," New York Times, October 9, 1994. Copyright ©1994 by The New York Times Company. Reprinted by permission.

Jacqueline Engel Irwin quit her job as a marketing director at Citibank in 1980 to raise her two daughters. Eight years later, after running her own consulting firm and starting an after-school center, she returned to corporate life in a position for which she felt overqualified. Ms. Irwin, 52, spent six years at the Nynex Corporation in New York, retracing her steps up the corporate ladder. In terms of salary and responsibilities, she figures she is no further along than when she stepped off the fast track in 1980.

Kitty Knecht began paving the road back to the fast track on the day that she announced her second pregnancy. A market researcher at the Quaker Oats Company in Chicago, she received a commitment from management to let her come back part time—three days a week—after her maternity leave. When she was ready for a full-time schedule two years later in 1991, she negotiated a promotion as a condition for the increased work load. But Ms. Knecht, who has a Ph.D. in psychology, still landed in what looked like a dead-end job. She said she sensed a need "to prove that I would travel, that I could stand the pace, that I could be productive and that I wasn't going to get pregnant again." Ms. Knecht, 41, has since earned another promotion.

Celeste Robb-Nicholson, a Boston physician with four children, worked four days a week for six years—first at Brigham and Women's Hospital and more recently at Massachusetts General. Both hospitals offered her tremendous flexibility, she said. But when Dr. Robb-Nicholson, 44, switched in 1993 to a full-time schedule, she found that she would not earn as much as peers who had consistently worked full time.

BACK FROM THE SIDELINES

Ms. Irwin, Ms. Knecht and Dr. Robb-Nicholson were part of the first great wave of women to enter business and the professions during the 1970's. A decade later, with careers well under way, many women in this group cut back or took a break for childcare reasons. Now, some of them are leading a new wave of the 90's: women working their way back from the sidelines and the mommy track.

The experiences of Ms. Irwin and the others reflect those of many women making the return trip. For all the talk by companies about accommodating work and family needs, not much has really changed, employment experts say.

"The traditional managerial career path of a continued uninterrupted climb up the corporate ladder is still held in high regard," said Joy Schneer, associate professor of management at Rider University's College of Business Administration in Lawrenceville, N.J. "If you violate that, there are repercussions."

PAINFUL TRADE-OFFS

Patricia Caputo, who worked up until the day her daughter was born and returned 12 weeks later, puts it bluntly: "You either make the decision to stick it out on the fast track or you drop out and you don't get back on. There's a big talent pool out there, and you're easily replaced." Ms. Caputo was promoted to senior business unit manager at the consumer pharmaceuticals division of the Ciba-Geigy Corporation in Woodbridge, N.J., soon after returning in 1992. At age 39 and pregnant again, she is not sure she would have received the promotion if she had taken even a few more months off.

Many of the women who chose to scale back have experienced painful trade-offs. Women like Ms. Irwin, who measure their time off in years, have had to pay their dues all over again. And, to a lesser degree, so have women like Ms. Knecht and Dr. Robb-Nicholson, even though they cut back only slightly.

The stories of these women may not surprise people who expect that taking a break will have opportunity costs. All's fair in work and family, they argue: Women who choose to step off the fast track should not complain when peers who kept moving outpace them. Besides, the argument continues, working parents with the financial flexibility to take time off are a privileged group.

SHODDY TREATMENT FOR WORKING MOTHERS

But many women who try to pick up where they left off say the dues they must pay go beyond catching up on seniority and honing rusty skills. Often, they say, there is a petty and punitive edge: People who take time off risk being treated virtually as beginners, or, even worse, as dilettantes, no matter how broad their experience. Even women who keep careers afloat by cutting just one day a week may forever lag behind in salary, title and responsibilities

Surprising or not, the early reports from those who came back could have profound implications for American companies, employment experts say. Discouraged by the news from the front, more women may forgo taking a break, risking early burnout. And more of those who do take a break may decide not to try a comeback, causing business to suffer a "brain drain" of experienced female professionals.

Such a loss would add to the costs already associated with the glass ceiling, the pervasive, often subtle, barriers to advancement that hold back many women from top positions. Such barriers are keeping the economy from growing to its full potential, [then] Labor Secretary Robert B. Reich said in September 1994 at a hearing of the Government's Glass Ceiling Commission.

DISCRIMINATION AGAINST MOTHERS

Deborah Swiss and Judith Walker, the authors of *Women and the Work/Family Dilemma*, cite the examples of a woman whose clients were reassigned to others only because she announced she was having a baby and another who was told by a male mentor, "Take my advice. Don't take your whole maternity leave. Not if you want to keep your job." Several women had their babies on Friday and returned to work on Monday for fear their standing at work would be jeopardized. One lawyer who took four months off was greeted upon her return with a monthly billing report highlighting a $40,000 loss in income because of her absence. An obstetrician said she was asked to be assistant chief of her hospital department, but the offer was withdrawn when she announced she was pregnant.

Priscilla Painton, Time, May 10, 1993.

No one knows just how many women drop out for child-care reasons—or how many try to get back in. The one hard fact is that women constitute an ever-growing percentage of American workers, up from 44.7 percent in 1973 to 57.9 percent in 1993.

Many women now re-entering the job market have adjusted their expectations before. They came of age professionally believing the myth of superwoman, that high-octane executive who juggled career and family without breaking a sweat. One by one, women reluctantly confessed that they could not live up to this model.

BACK ON THE FAST TRACK

To be sure, some businesses have made it easier for them by becoming more flexible about schedules, permitting employees to work part time, telecommute or share jobs with other working parents.

But these opportunities, which are still relatively rare, are often reserved for women who "were already the high performers, the very valued employees," said Kathleen Christensen, an environmental psychology professor in the graduate program of the City University of New York who has tracked workplace and family trends. "Companies have been allowing it largely because they don't want to lose this person and because they want them back on the fast track."

Victoria Brooks, a vice president at J.P. Morgan & Company, for example, worked four days a week for seven years when her children were young, and is now back full time, heading the company's global training program. Resuming a full-time schedule "happened pretty easily," said Ms. Brooks, 48. She attributes her smooth transition two years ago to the fact that she had a 17-year track record with the company.

A Rough Road

But for many women, the road is much rougher. Although Ms. Irwin had an M.B.A. from the University of Chicago, 12 years of experience in managerial jobs at major corporations and had run a lucrative business of her own, a headhunter prepared her for a comedown when she started job hunting again in 1988. She should expect to earn no more than she made at her last corporate post eight years earlier, he said. As a vice president in charge of marketing at Citibank, Ms. Irwin's 1980 salary had been $60,000.

Ms. Irwin re-entered the work force at a lower level, as a marketing specialist for Nynex. Ultimately, she was able to get a promotion and make several lateral job changes.

Today she is staff director of market planning in the company's New York offices. Her current salary, she said, is less than her 1980 salary adjusted for inflation. Large companies "have molds," Ms. Irwin said. "It is very hard for them to deal with someone who is out of the mold."

Ms. Knecht has tried to work within the mold at Quaker Oats. By promising management that she would come back full time eventually, she framed her request for part-time work "as an investment the company was going to make in me that they were going to be paid back for," she said. To help her prospects for promotion after she returned, she "volunteered for some high-profile good works," like leading the United Way drive in her department and serving on a benefits design team.

The strategy worked: two years later, Ms. Knecht got a promotion to her current position as director of Quaker's convenience foods division. Like Ms. Irwin, though, she thinks she would be further along and making more money had there been no interruption.

Sacrificing Career Advancement

A study by Professor Schneer of Rider University of the career paths of M.B.A.'s suggests that women executives who take time off and later go back to work permanently sacrifice career advancement and earning potential. In her study, with Frieda Reitman, professor emeritus at Pace University's Lubin School of Business in Pleasantville, N.Y., Ms. Schneer compared 128 women who had never had a gap in their employment with 63 who had taken time off and gone back to work full time by 1987.

The researchers were dealing with women who had relatively brief interruptions—an average of 8.8 months. After adjusting for differences like years of experience, the study found that women who took a break earned 17 percent less in 1993 than women who didn't. Sixty percent of the women without a gap in employment had reached upper-middle management or higher; for those with a gap, only 44 percent reached that level.

Both groups were equally satisfied with their careers, however. Ms. Schneer speculates that women adjusted their goals so that they were happy with less.

PART-TIME POSSIBILITIES

Although Dr. Robb-Nicholson finds her career fulfilling, she is not happy with the dollars-and-cents trade-off that is a legacy of her years on a four-day week.

Part-time work has become more acceptable, she said, but it still has different connotations to different people. While young women professionals feel encouraged by the growing number of part-time opportunities, older colleagues may label part-time professionals as dabblers. "The uncertainty of returning," Dr. Robb-Nicholson said, is "what will your act have meant to whomever it is you are trying to get a job with?"

Bettina B. Plevan, a partner at the law firm of Proskauer Rose Goetz & Mendelsohn in New York, returned to work within two weeks after her second child was born in the mid-1970s and stayed on the fast track throughout her career. Ms. Plevan now makes hiring and promotion decisions about women lawyers who have opted for reduced work schedules.

While it is not impossible for someone who worked part time to become a partner at the firm, "it's difficult to maintain the degree of interest and dedication to the job the more time you're away from the office," Ms. Plevan said. People who put families first are making "a legitimate choice," she added. But "for a period of time at least, maybe forever, the job is secondary."

> "It's not cartoonishly chauvinistic
> male bosses who hold women back,
> but the impinging nature of
> motherhood itself."

WORKING MOTHERS ARE NOT DISCRIMINATED AGAINST

Danielle Crittenden

In the following viewpoint, Danielle Crittenden argues that working mothers experience limited opportunities and lower wages not because they are discriminated against, but because raising children often requires women to take time off from work. Women who work fewer hours because of motherhood should not expect to obtain the same raises and promotions that men earn, she maintains. Crittenden is editor of the *Women's Quarterly*, a conservative journal published by the Independent Women's Forum.

As you read, consider the following questions:

1. According to June O'Neill, as quoted by Crittenden, how do the earnings of women who have never had a child compare with men's earnings?
2. In the author's opinion, why do mothers suffer more than fathers when they leave their children in day care?
3. What is the "mommy track," according to Crittenden?

My tax return for 1991, the year my first child was born, shows that I earned a whopping $800. Fortunately, my husband earned somewhat more that year. We were not sent to the workhouse. But did my lack of income make me "unequal" to him?

My meager earnings, after all, defied 20 years of government policy designed to keep me in the work force—from the pressure put on companies to hire and promote me, to guaranteed maternity leave, to the tax code's marriage penalty. By letting my earnings trail off (not, I add, that they were so royal to begin with), I contributed to the depressing Census Bureau statistic that women earn 76 percent of what men do.

MISUSED STATISTICS

Feminists—from the halls of the United Nations to the research offices of the Labor Department—appear to believe that until women's earnings climb to 100 percent of men's, we cannot truthfully say we live in a just society. They swing this 76 percent statistic the way an old-fashioned policeman used his nightstick, to club all opposition into silence.

They also resist evidence that casts doubt on their grievances, like the striking finding of the economist June O'Neill, director of the Congressional Budget Office, that women have achieved the magical, statistical parity with men in the work force—so long as they don't become mothers.

Ms. O'Neill reports that "among women and men aged 27 to 33, who have never had a child, the earnings of women in the National Longitudinal Survey of Youth are close to 98 percent of men's." It's the vast majority of us who become mothers who are responsible for dragging the average down.

MOST WOMEN WANT TO BE MOTHERS

What is so subversive about Ms. O'Neill's finding—subversive, at least, to advocates of workplace parity—is that it demonstrates that it's not cartoonishly chauvinistic male bosses who hold women back, but the impinging nature of motherhood itself.

To these advocates, Ms. O'Neill's research no doubt demonstrates the need for more of the programs they champion—rigorously enforced affirmative action, government-subsidized day care and the like—so women may pursue the rewards of the work force unhindered, just like men. But the question advocates dare not ask is: Is this what women want?

A more realistic conclusion to be drawn from the O'Neill findings is that, despite two decades of policies and social pressure urging them to do otherwise, the majority of women still need and want to mother their children. No amount of government aid and regulation, no system of state-supported baby-sitting, will offset biological fact: the cry of a baby is more compelling than the call of the office.

WOMEN'S CHOICES

There are still far fewer women than men in senior management positions, but feminists don't acknowledge that this disparity is at least partly the result of women's choices. Women with children, for example, often want to work fewer hours than men, and some mothers prefer to channel their ambition into their family rather than into a job.

Laura A. Ingraham, *New York Times*, April 19, 1995.

Those of us who are mothers don't need studies to prove that having a child affects even the most insanely ambitious among us, and affects us differently from our husbands. This doesn't mean a woman has to abandon her career. But giving birth will certainly constrain it. Maybe some women will have to go right back to work, and others will want to. Some will prefer to stay home during their children's early years or to work part time, and others still will drop out of the work force entirely. But no woman will be unaffected by the birth of her child.

UNFAIRNESS TO MOTHERS?

Is this unfair? Probably. But it is an issue to take up with nature, not Congress. And I'm not even sure I'd wish to argue with nature. Experts are just beginning to acknowledge the unhealthiness of day-care-from-birth; I know working mothers who have "the best nannies in the world" and yet are collapsing under the mental strain of walking out the door every morning (a strain, by the way, which their husbands, thanks to their genetic wiring, blissfully do not suffer). Until advocates of workplace parity accept that women wish to be with their children—and that this is not a bad thing—the discussion will never move from its rut in statistics toward measures that might be truly helpful. Among them might be the much-derided "mommy track," which would accommodate career women who want to take time out or work less at the price of lower wages and slower advancement.

So let me go back to my original question: Did my $800 tax return make me unequal to my husband? Let's see. He put on suit and tie every morning; I wore something splatter-proof. He left the house with a briefcase; I left with a stroller. He faced the demands of his colleagues and bosses; I was subject to the somewhat more insistent demands of an infant ("Your boss," I once spat at him, "at least lets you go to the bathroom"). He lay awake at night balancing the household expenses in his head; I lay awake, balancing the next day's schedules.

If we are the sum of our tasks, and the tasks of a mother are valued less by society than the tasks of an employee, then yes, I am unequal. But I'd like to think that a progressive society is one which understands that not everything worthwhile pays off in cash.

| *"Affirmative action policies have been largely responsible for bringing women into jobs and professions from which they were previously excluded."*

WOMEN NEED AFFIRMATIVE ACTION TO OVERCOME DISCRIMINATION

Ann Menasche

Affirmative action policies are designed to ensure that jobs are accessible to qualified people regardless of their gender or race. In the following viewpoint, Ann Menasche argues that these policies, which she says have increased employment opportunities for women in the last three decades of the twentieth century, remain necessary to help eliminate discrimination against working women. According to Menasche, women still need affirmative action to counter continuing pay inequities, sexual harassment, maltreatment, and gender bias in the workplace. Menasche is a civil rights lawyer in San Francisco, California.

As you read, consider the following questions:

1. According to Menasche, what were the justifications for excluding women from jobs traditionally held by males?
2. What percentage of working women earn less than $20,000 a year, according to the author?
3. According to the "results-based standard" described by Menasche, what is the cause of gender inequities in the workplace?

From Ann Menasche, "Women and Affirmative Action," *Independent Politics*, November/December 1995. Reprinted with permission.

Most opponents of affirmative action have characterized the issue as solely one of race. They have done so consciously in order to exploit the fear and ignorance of the white population and to thereby drive a wedge against African-Americans and other persons of color. Such attempts at "divide and conquer" are a lot less effective, however, when it is recognized that affirmative action is also about gender. Women, too, need affirmative action.

OPEN DOORS FOR WOMEN

Affirmative action policies have been largely responsible for bringing women into jobs and professions from which they were previously excluded. Two or three decades ago, there were no women firefighters, airline pilots, news anchors, or women in the skilled trades; women doctors, lawyers, judges, and college professors were a rarity when they existed at all. Help wanted ads were divided between "men's jobs" and "women's jobs"; with the women's jobs, of course, having the lowest pay, status, and opportunities for advancement.

Young girls were actively discouraged from pursuing "unfeminine" careers (anything that might interfere with their primary role as wives and mothers), or from developing too much intellectual or athletic ability that might "threaten" the boys. In 1963, when I was in junior high school, I had the fantasy of becoming a forest ranger. My school provided me with a pamphlet stating that a girl couldn't become a forest ranger (it was just too difficult for a girl) but she needn't be disappointed since she could still "marry one."

The justification for keeping women in their place was that men had greater innate abilities in certain areas than women did; that women were weaker, less competitive, less intelligent (less good in math and abstract thinking), than men and that men were and always would be "more qualified" for all the important work of the world. Women were, on the other hand, "naturally" gifted at nurturing, typing, and menial work, and should be satisfied with such work, even if it didn't pay very well or at all.

Certainly, things have improved for women since then—more women work outside the home and more women have broken through to fields traditionally reserved for men. None of this was accidental. The mass mobilizations of the civil rights and feminist movements of the sixties and seventies, the passage of the 1964 Civil Rights Act, and numerous lawsuits and consent decrees, all forced government and industry to go beyond the "old boys' network" for hiring, to do real outreach, training, and promotion of women, and to take other proactive measures to bring women into positions that had been closed to them. Such "affirmative action" or "preferences" were merely efforts to equalize the playing field in a world that had been stacked against women for centuries.

SLOWED PROGRESS

However, by the late 1970s with the U.S. Supreme Court's *Regents of the University of California v. Allan Bakke* decision, affirmative action was already being weakened. "Quotas"—which are nothing but affirmative action with teeth—were outlawed, and any preferences for minorities were to be strictly scrutinized by the same test used to judge the legality of discrimination *against* disadvantaged groups. Progress toward genuine equality began to slow down.

In addition, women were often not given a warm welcome by male bosses and coworkers when they arrived in previously male work environments. Rather, severe sexual harassment, including physical assault and death threats, was the common experience of the courageous pioneering women who, by the ones and twos, broke into the trades and other "male" jobs in the 1970s and 1980s. According to California NOW [National Organization for Women], state agencies with a greater proportion of men to women continue to have higher reported incidents of sexual harassment. Some women were and continue to be forced out of these jobs by such treatment.

WOMEN EARN LESS

Despite the myth that we are now living in a "meritocracy," that women are already "liberated," and that if anyone is suffering from discrimination, it is white males, the reality is quite different. Women still earn only 72 percent as much as males do for comparable jobs. Equal Rights Advocates estimates that 70 percent of 57 million working women in the U.S. earn less than $20,000 per year and 40 percent earn less than $10,000 per year. And African-American and Hispanic women earn significantly less than white women. This means that millions of working women, especially women of color, lesbians, and unmarried heterosexual women, are living in poverty.

As the standard of living and buying power of all workers goes down, and jobs that pay a living wage become harder to come by, women are among the hardest hit. Meanwhile, the measly safety net of welfare is being removed from single and divorced mothers, who are left with few options for survival outside of heterosexual marriage.

Less than half of the male-female wage gap is accounted for by differences in education and experience. A Latina woman with a college degree still earns less, on average, than a white man with a high school diploma. Where women have managed to get into higher status jobs and professions, the male-female wage gap has continued to exist and often *increases*. For example, 74 percent of women professors at the University of California at Davis earn less than their male colleagues with the same years of experience and qualifications.

DRESS FOR SUCCESS

Reprinted by permission of Kirk Anderson.

And despite the undeniable progress since the 1950s and 60s, the workforce remains, by and large, sex segregated, with women concentrated in the low-wage sectors. More than nine out of ten workers in such low-paying occupations as secretaries, nurses, bookkeepers, accounting clerks and child care providers are women.

Men continue to dominate high paying fields such as architects, engineers, physicians, lawyers and judges, police and firefighters and skilled crafts. Women in California are 14 percent of judges, 11 percent of full professors, 10 percent of college and university presidents, and over 73 percent of teachers at the elementary and secondary school level.

No matter how you look at it, the gains for women made under the impetus of affirmative action have been extremely modest. For example, women were barred from the San Francisco Fire Department until 1978. The first women were hired in 1987 due to court-ordered affirmative action. Today there are a total of 70–75 women out of a force of about 1,500. Similarly, at UC Davis in 1990–1992, a mere 27 percent of faculty hires were women; only white men continue to be hired there, at rates higher than their availability in the qualified Ph.D. pool. Given the same credentials, it is still easier for men than women to secure academic jobs.

Despite years of affirmative action, companies owned by white males continue to receive the vast majority of public contracts with the State of California and City of Los Angeles. A *Los Angeles Times* examination of affirmative action awards of government contracts in California found that such programs are generally ineffective. "Old boys'" networks have found ways to subvert the process by which women and minorities could participate, while court decisions have severely limited what public agencies could do to ensure that women and minorities received their fair share. "Even with affirmative action, we're only getting crumbs," said Latino State Senator Richard G. Polanco.

And then there is the notorious "glass-ceiling" that keeps white men at the top of economic and political power. According to the Glass Ceiling Report sponsored by Republican members of Congress, women hold between 3 and 5 percent of senior management positions in the nation's largest companies. In Congress, the percentage of female representation is equally dismal. The degree of resistance and hostility to the admission of women to the Citadel military academy symbolizes the all-pervading and institutionalized nature of discrimination against women in this society.

IN WOMEN'S TRUE INTERESTS

What women need is more, not less affirmative action. Women need to be trained and hired in large numbers for jobs and professions that have previously had few or no women. Laws against sexual harassment must be vigorously enforced. Girls in school need to be given special assistance (including experiments in all-girl classes) in learning math and science, and in gaining confidence in themselves to speak up and act in the world.

The alternative of fighting sex discrimination through individual lawsuits or discrimination claims is like attempting to drain the ocean with a spoon. Proving intentional discrimination one instance at a time is never easy and always expensive. Sometimes discrimination is not intentional but simply a result of centuries of doing things a certain way. What we need is a results-based standard which is what affirmative action is all about. A results-based standard says that if women are not equally represented in this job or profession, if men are paid more than women, this is a result of the sexist prejudices of the culture, not because women can't or won't do the job, or that their work has inherently less value. And this state of affairs must be corrected. Without affirmative action, the male-dominated status quo will be frozen in place forever. The rationale will be, as before, that women are simply "less qualified"; in a word, "inferior."

All women, white women included, clearly have a powerful interest in defending and strengthening affirmative action. Educating and mobilizing women in defense of their true interests is key to building a coalition with people of color, and enlightened white men that can help turn back the backlash and move us forward again.

> "The American working woman pays
> a high price for the position . . . she
> receives from affirmative action: the
> unspoken assumption that she was
> not the 'best man' for the job."

WOMEN DO NOT NEED AFFIRMATIVE ACTION

Elizabeth Larson

In the following viewpoint, Elizabeth Larson contends that women do not need affirmative action policies to ensure employment and success in the workplace. According to Larson, these policies can actually be harmful because they grant preferential treatment to women as a group and create the assumption that female employees are not truly qualified for their positions. Women have made many gains in occupations traditionally held by men, Larson argues. Moreover, she concludes, the success of female entrepreneurs who are running their own companies suggests that women do not need government-sanctioned affirmative action. Larson is a Los Angeles–based writer who has published many articles about women in the workplace.

As you read, consider the following questions:

1. According to Larson, what is the reason for the continuing "wage gap" between male and female workers?
2. What are some well-known companies that are run by women, according to the author?
3. In Larson's opinion, why is it wrong to promote group rights over individual rights?

From Elizabeth Larson, "No Thanks, Uncle Sam," *Freeman*, December 1995. Reprinted by permission of the *Freeman*. Endnotes in the original article have been omitted.

Today's businesswoman needs affirmative action like a fish needs a bicycle.

With two important developments in the affirmative-action battle in the summer of 1995—the Supreme Court's decision in *Adarand v. Pena* and the vote by the University of California Board of Regents to discontinue affirmative-action policies for student admissions—an optimist might assume this last universal barrier to women's advancement in the workplace is finally about to topple. Yet victories over policies that are not just misguided but morally wrong must be won at the intellectual level as well as the practical.

Until now, the framework for discussing women in the workplace has been set by feminists—activists who will not be silent until 51 percent of every job classification is filled by women. These same radicals are willing to wave aside the achievements of the individual for the collectivist utopia of group success. Hence the urgency of the struggle over affirmative action at the intellectual level. Though they profess to—and perhaps believe it as well—these activists do not voice the beliefs and interests of most American women. It is time to reclaim the debate, reminding ourselves of the costs women have borne because of affirmative action as well as its danger to liberty.

PAYING A HIGH PRICE

The American working woman pays a high price for the position or promotion she receives from affirmative action: the unspoken assumption that she was not the "best man" for the job. At a teach-in on affirmative action at the University of California–Los Angeles (UCLA), one of the participants *defending* affirmative action provided the best example of how the policy foments these very questions about competence.

Ellen DuBois, a full professor of history at UCLA and the author of such books on women's history as *Feminism and Suffrage: The Emergence of an Independent Women's Movement in the U.S., 1848–1869*, and the co-author of *Unequal Sisters: A Multicultural Reader in U.S. Women's History*, began her comments by describing herself to the audience as "an affirmative-action baby—and proud of it." She explained how her first job after graduate school was at the State University of New York, thanks to the school's new affirmative-action policy, and continued with: "When I was first listening to the claims of the Civil Rights Initiative people, my parents were with me, and I said to them, 'You know, I was an affirmative-action appointment.' And they said, 'Oh! But you *deserved* your job.' And I thought that that sort of captured everything—the assumption that I, the one they know, deserve my job, but all the rest of these people who have affirmative-action positions don't deserve their jobs. It's just an accident that their dear daughter did."

BREEDING DISCRIMINATION

Suspicions about the merits of those who receive affirmative-action jobs are often undeserved, and thus all the more insidious. When the suspicions are held by one's colleagues, rather than the general public, it is particularly divisive. Resentment against an individual case of hiring by quota ferments into resentment against all members of the privileged group. Intended to reverse discrimination, affirmative action eventually breeds it. The supporters of such a perverse system must answer the question of how successful—and more importantly, how *moral*—a system is that harms the very individuals it purports to help.

Unfortunately, concrete concerns and real-life reservations about affirmative action are commonly dismissed as anecdotal—and, indeed, it is difficult to quantify such arguments with numbers. So let us turn to the actual statistics used to "prove" the need for affirmative-action programs.

THE WAGE GAP

It turns out that supporters of affirmative action would have us level the playing field in all areas except the reporting of statistics. The infamous wage gap is so common a refrain that it approaches cliché. On closer inspection, however, the gap shown by all the "data" is neither as wide nor as unbridgeable as it is portrayed. Once you stop lumping all women of all ages in all fields together and using that resulting dollar figure as representative of the average American working woman, the gap narrows.

Comparing the wages of women and men of the same age, with similar experience, training, and years of uninterrupted time in their field yields a much more optimistic picture of how women fare today. Women under age 20 earn 92 percent as much as their male counterparts, women 21 to 24 earn 85 percent, and women 25 to 34 earn 78 percent. The younger the group, the slimmer the difference, suggesting that the wage gap will eventually disappear.

According to a report from the U.S. Civil Rights Commission, the gaps that do still exist are likely due to the fewer continuous years women have been in the workforce. Women who have never interrupted their careers for any reason now earn at least 98 percent as much as their male counterparts.

In addition to painting a picture using tendentious numbers, many feminists labor under assumptions about the workplace and the meaning of success that are both unreasonable and unrealistic. They seem to believe that making an attempt at her job in and of itself guarantees a woman success. Yet the free market that has given women opportunities to work outside of the home that are unparalleled in history is the same free market that does not hand out "A's" for effort. Just because a woman wants to be the first female CEO of her company does not mean she is entitled to the position, or that if she fails to make it that far up the corporate ladder it is someone else's fault. Luck, drive, brains, connections, education, and, yes, looks, can all play a part in the promotions any worker—male, or female—receives.

ECONOMIC REALITIES

A look at the role of physical attractiveness in determining wages exemplifies just how unrealistic feminists are when it comes to success in the workplace. Using American and Canadian subjects, economists Daniel Hamermesh and Jeff Biddle found that, even after adjusting for education and other factors, very attractive men and women earn about 5 percent more per hour than their merely average-looking colleagues. Plain women earn 5 percent less than the average-looking workers, and plain men 10 percent less. It seems that when the beauty myth becomes economic reality, men have even more to complain about than women.

FREE-MARKET SUCCESS STORIES

If feminists truly cared about women succeeding rather than constructing a social utopia, they would herald individual women who have genuine, free-market success stories to tell. These women are not running to government for affirmative-action privilege because they are too busy running companies.

Jane Hirsh is one such woman. Today one of the country's wealthiest businesswomen, Hirsh founded Copley Pharmaceutical Inc. more than two decades ago because she wanted to be able to bring her children to work. After 21 years spent building her company into a generic-drug powerhouse, Hirsh sold a 51 percent stake in Copley to the German company Hoechst for $546 million in cash in 1993, retaining 37 percent of the shares for her family. Starting her own company "was the only way I could have a crib in my office," Hirsh recalled.

Edith Gorter of Gorter Express Company has her own hard-work success story to tell. She was one of seven female entrepreneurs that author and businesswoman Joline Godfrey chose to highlight in her book on businesswomen, *Our Wildest Dreams*. Gorter took over the trucking company when her brother-in-law who had been running it died. (Her husband, who had no head for business, had wanted to sell the family company, founded by his father in 1910 with a horse and wagon.) When Edith Gorter took the company's reins in 1972, Gorter Express had just one client, two trucks, and little else. Today, the company has hundreds of clients and about $2 million in rolling stock. Her daughter Lori seems the likely candidate to take over the company from her mother.

Preferences Are Wrong

[One] reason why affirmative action is wrong is that the woman receiving the benefit is not a woman who was discriminated against. Nobody should be entitled to receive a remedy for an injury suffered by someone else. Women are not a monolithic, cohesive community in which a grievance suffered by one woman can be remedied by a preference given to another woman.

Phyllis Schlafly, *Conservative Chronicle*, April 4, 1995.

Little Caesar's pizza chain, Mrs. Field's Cookies, and Ruth's Chris Steakhouses are a few of the better-known companies founded or run by women, but there are literally thousands of great free-market success stories like these. In fact, more than 6.5 million American businesses are owned by women. As a recent Associated Press story reported: "From 1991 to 1994, woman-owned businesses in the transportation, communications, wholesale trade, real estate and financial services grew nearly 20 percent, while construction firms grew 19 percent and manufacturing firms 13 percent, according to the National Foundation for Women Business Owners." Since women start their own companies with half as much capital as men do, these entrepreneurs do not have the luxury of free time to complain about perceived workplace inequalities.

Striking Gains for Women

Some might argue that while entrepreneurial women have the opportunity to pick their field, most female workers are still forced to do "women's work." Although about two-thirds of working women still enter traditionally female fields such as nursing, teaching, and social work, a study from the Population Reference Bureau found "striking gains" for women in such traditionally male fields as medicine and law during the 1980s. The number of women lawyers more than tripled, and the number of female doctors doubled. Since the "decade of greed" was supposedly even worse for women than for men, this is good news.

GROUP VERSUS INDIVIDUAL RIGHTS

It is important to note that the debate about affirmative action is not a debate about the existence of individuals who discriminate on the basis of sex, nor should it be. Like the poor, the misogynist will always be with us. What differentiates the sexist society from a free society in which there is sexism is whether that prejudice is sanctioned by legislation and government policies or whether it is forced to the margins of society by general condemnation.

The affirmative-action debate is ultimately an argument about group versus individual rights. Affirmative action's opponents understand that it is wrong, and not merely impractical, to restrain the individual for the sake of the group. They know from history that to ignore or denigrate the achievements of the individual is to head society down the road to chaos. The factional fighting that ensues is not of the beneficent type described by the Founders, wherein special interests jostle amongst themselves creating a balance from which everyone's rights emerge intact. It is a splintering of communities born of contempt and resentment. Liberty has no friends in a world where success is seen as an entitlement, for the politically strong do what they can to obtain this "right" while the politically weak suffer what they must.

WOMEN SHOULD NOT RELY ON GOVERNMENT

Feminists ought to be particularly attuned to the dangers of relying on a central force or figure for support and protection. Women struggled far too long to free themselves from paternalism to hold the hand of Uncle Sam now. An eagerness to rely on the government is an affront to what feminism should stand for. It betrays a lack of confidence in women's abilities to achieve financial and personal independence, and it undermines the real gains women have made in the workplace in recent decades.

As with any group that considers itself the vanguard of a brave new world, feminists want immediate change—and affirmative-action programs with the force of bureaucratic edict promise it to them. Yet utopias are malleable things. Just as the dream of a color-blind society has become the reality of a color-coded one since the passage of the 1964 Civil Rights Act, the goal of equal opportunity has become the mirage of equal outcome. A system in which less than 5 percent of construction jobs are held by women—even though women own almost as many construction companies as men—is a system which, to many feminists, has failed the fairer sex.

But try telling that to someone like Edith Gorter—who hasn't just made it in a "man's world"; she's made it in a man's field, trucking. Where are the feminists to praise strong, independent women when you need them? Running after yet another gift from the government sugar daddy.

PERIODICAL BIBLIOGRAPHY

The following articles have been selected to supplement the diverse views presented in this chapter. Addresses are provided for periodicals not indexed in the *Readers' Guide to Periodical Literature*, the *Alternative Press Index*, the *Social Sciences Index*, or the *Index to Legal Periodicals and Books*.

Eugenie Allen	"Surviving Diversity Training," *Working Woman*, September 1995.
Mary Becker and Patricia A. Casey	"Sex Discrimination," *ABA Journal*, February 1996.
Diana Bilimoira and Sandy Kristin Piderit	"Sexism on High: Corporate Boards," *New York Times*, February 5, 1995.
Laura Dresser	"To Be Young, Black, and Female: Falling Further Behind in the Shifting Economy," *Dollars and Sense*, May/June 1995.
Tom Dunkel	"Affirmative Reaction," *Working Woman*, October 1995.
Glamour	"Are White Men *Really* Oppressed?" May 1995.
Glamour	"Equal Opportunity?" August 1996.
Laura A. Ingraham	"Enter, Women," *New York Times*, April 19, 1995.
Anthony Layng	"Tracing the Roots of Sexual Discrimination," *USA Today*, September 1993.
Joann S. Lublin	"Firms Designate Some Openings for Women Only," *Wall Street Journal*, February 7, 1994.
Priscilla Painton	"The Maternal Wall," *Time*, May 10, 1993.
Katie Roiphe	"The Independent Woman (and Other Lies)," *Esquire*, February 1997.
Elizabeth Roth	"The Civil Rights History of 'Sex,'" *Ms.*, March/April 1993.
Terri Scandura	"Women Can Shatter Job Barriers," *USA Today*, May 1994.
Rochelle Sharpe	"The Waiting Game," *Wall Street Journal*, March 29, 1994.
Peter Steinfels	"Vatican Says the Ban on Women As Priests Is 'Infallible' Doctrine," *New York Times*, November 19, 1995.

Deborah Tannen	"Wears Jump Suit. Sensible Shoes. Uses Husband's Last Name," *New York Times Magazine,* June 20, 1993.
Joan Walsh	"Can Diversity Training Move Them Up?" *Glamour,* November 1995.
Sheila Wellington	"Women Are in the Wrong Conduits," *Vital Speeches of the Day,* December 15, 1996.

CHAPTER 3

HOW SERIOUS A PROBLEM IS SEXUAL HARASSMENT IN THE WORKPLACE?

CHAPTER PREFACE

Since the fall of 1992, when law professor Anita Hill testified during Supreme Court confirmation hearings that Judge Clarence Thomas had sexually harassed her when she worked for him years before, sexual harassment has been a topic of debate nationwide. Many commentators applaud Hill for focusing national attention on a problem that they believe is prevalent in America's workplaces. Others insist that due to Hill's testimony, the behavior of employees has been excessively scrutinized for signs of inappropriate words and actions.

This increased attention to the issue of sexual harassment has been accompanied by a spate of sexual harassment claims, some of which have resulted in large financial settlements for the plaintiffs. In an attempt to avoid such costly litigation, many companies have instituted policies and programs—including gender sensitivity training, reporting procedures, and disciplinary guidelines—designed to prevent sexual harassment. Critics contend that these efforts constitute an excessive response to a minor problem. According to attorney Ellen Wagner, "Companies are overreacting [to sexual harassment]. Accusers are believed on the basis of very little evidence or none at all. And the ultimate punishment, termination, is a first resort rather than last one."

However, many legal experts and women in business argue that antiharassment policies are an appropriate response to a serious problem. As a consequence of sexual harassment, they maintain, many women have lost promotions, raises, and jobs and have suffered physical and emotional problems. These commentators insist that the new policies adopted by business are necessary in order to protect women from abuse and discrimination and to create more cooperative and productive workplaces. As the general counsel for the U.S. Chamber of Commerce, Bruce Bokat, puts it, "Let's face it, sexual harassment does not add to the bottom line, and a really sophisticated company now has a lot of guidelines that are easy to comply with."

Whether the debate over sexual harassment has harmed or benefited businesses and working women is among the issues discussed in the following chapter on the extent of sexual harassment in the workplace.

|"Sexual harassment in the workplace is a problem. After all, men have been harassing women for ages."

SEXUAL HARASSMENT IS A SERIOUS PROBLEM

L.A. Winokur

Public attention became focused on sexual harassment in the fall of 1991 when Anita Hill accused Supreme Court nominee Clarence Thomas of sexually harassing her several years before. In the following viewpoint, L.A. Winokur argues that the Hill-Thomas hearings revealed the extent and severity of sexual harassment in the workplace. Sexual harassment is a serious problem, she contends, both because so many women have experienced it and because it makes women feel angry, uncomfortable, and ashamed at work. Women are often forced to choose between coping with harassment at their workplace because they need the job security and the income or trying to find a new job in order to escape the harassment, Winokur asserts. Winokur is a writer in Atlanta and a contributor to the *Progressive*, a monthly liberal journal of news and opinion.

As you read, consider the following questions:

1. According to Winokur, how do women react physically and emotionally to sexual harassment in the workplace?
2. Winokur states, "Sexual harassment isn't about sex." What does she say it is about?
3. Why are many women reluctant to report sexual harassment, according to the author?

From L.A. Winokur, "The Sexual-Harassment Debates," *Progressive*, November 1993. Reprinted by permission of the author.

Let's face it. It didn't take Anita Hill's coming forward for the rest of us women to know that sexual harassment in the workplace is a problem. After all, men have been harassing women for ages. (It's still mostly men who do it.)

What Anita Hill did do, however—and for this, I think it would be fair to say, many women are grateful—was to give a more public voice to what once had been a little-talked-about topic.

THE LEGACY OF ANITA HILL

Witness the proliferation of books, newspaper and magazine articles, and broadcast reports on the subject, not to mention the I BELIEVE ANITA pins and bumper stickers that have cropped up since the Anita Hill–Clarence Thomas hearings in the fall of 1991. Also, stop and think for a moment about all of the women who have since come forward with their own stories of being victimized. It's become apparent how widespread the problem really is. Since the hearings, it seems that every time you turn around there's yet another sexual-harassment scandal in the news. For a while, it was the Navy's Tailhook convention. Then Senator Bob Packwood of Oregon stole the spotlight. [At the 1991 Tailhook Convention in Las Vegas, a number of military pilots sexually harassed and assaulted civilian and military women attending the convention. Bob Packwood was accused of sexual harassment by several former employees.]

Thanks to Anita Hill, I got the chance to throw my two cents into the ongoing media discussion as well as to try to come to terms personally with something that had happened to me several months before the Hill-Thomas hearings.

Eight months or so before the hearings, I had tried pitching a story on this subject to my editors. No dice, "We've done that before." After the hearings, I got to do my story.

As for the personal part: I was propositioned by a source—someone I regularly depend upon to get my job done. Whether or not it constituted harassment may be up for grabs, though I certainly know where I stand on the matter. Over drinks—a business meeting, I might add—he told me he had been wanting to sleep with me ever since he first met me. I wasn't flattered. Rather, I was stunned. For the next split second, which seemed like an eternity, my mind raced back over our three-year "relationship." Had I been too friendly? Too suggestive? Did I lead him on?

Then I became angry. All those years he had tipped me off to hot stories, and I thought it was because he thought I did a good job. Was it simply because he had hoped at some point to get me into the sack?

I made it clear to him that I wasn't interested and then changed the subject. And lucky for me, that's all it took to fend him off. But here it is, more than two years later, and that evening still comes back to haunt me.

Perhaps a public-relations executive summed it up best when, for a feature-length article I was working on, she told me about her experience of being harassed by a client. She said that even though she almost never spoke about what, to her, had been a humiliating experience—and it had happened twenty-five years before—"I remember it as if it were yesterday."

MEMORIES OF HARASSMENT

For countless numbers of women, the Hill-Thomas hearings opened the gates of denial, and long-repressed memories came tumbling out," note editors Amber Coverdale Sumrall and Dena Taylor, in their preface to *Sexual Harassment: Women Speak Out*. In this noteworthy book, an anthology of women's sexual-harassment stories dedicated to Anita Hill, with introductions by Andrea Dworkin and Margaret Randall, more than seventy women share their experiences and how they responded to them.

"Some went into extreme depression or experienced physical symptoms; some fought back; some denied the harassment was happening, wanting to believe it was unintentional or something they themselves provoked," the editors say.

Consider Carol Atkins, a writer who explains that, over the years, her response to harassment in the workplace has been simply to pick up and leave. "Even though it cost me jobs I liked, I left. I did not know that sexual harassment was endemic; I thought some other place would be free of it. I also thought that something in my behavior had triggered the harassment. . . . So I did not say anything to anyone about it, and used other reasons for leaving."

For Chris Karras, however, this was not an option. "My job supports me and my husband; I did not have the luxury of quitting, or looking elsewhere," says the office worker, who confesses that for years she was subjected to physical and verbal harassment from her boss.

"It always puzzles me when women are asked why we stay in a position when it is so unpleasant or even degrading," Karras continues. "Should I leave a paying job and wander from place to place because men have a behavior problem around women in the workplace?"

CONFUSION ABOUT SEXUAL HARASSMENT

At the moment, there's more confusion than ever over what is and isn't considered appropriate when it comes to communication and contact between the sexes. Women say men just don't get it. On the other hand, we've all heard male co-workers gripe about how this sexual-harassment business has gone too far; how they're afraid, say, to compliment a female colleague on a haircut or new outfit—let alone ask her out on a date—for fear of reprisal and of being branded a harasser.

"While most harassers are men, most men are not harassers," say Ellen Bravo, director of 9to5, and Ellen Cassedy in *The 9to5 Guide to Combating Sexual Harassment: Candid Advice from 9to5, the National Association of Working Women.* But some men, they maintain, are "truly confused by the changing times." They quote one man who complained that "unless you just keep your mouth shut, you're bound to make a remark that offends someone. Touch a woman's shoulder and you could be hauled into court."

"In a work world controlled by men," the authors note, "women have traditionally had to adjust to male expectations if they want to keep their jobs. Now men find that they are expected to modify their behavior to meet women's needs. While many find that the new rules aren't as arbitrary or complicated as they feared, others have difficulty accepting them."

AN ABUSE OF POWER

While staggering jury awards capture headlines, the truth is that few cases [of sexual harassment] ever find their way into a courtroom. Most victims suffer their humiliation in silence—pawns in an ugly game of power and intimidation that is played out in offices, on streets, in buses, at lunch counters, and in factories. At times, there is outright coercion to have intimate relations. Most of the time, though, the molestation consists of subtler, yet shamelessly offensive, acts: unwelcome or inappropriate touches, lewd remarks, lascivious stares.

Awake!, May 22, 1996.

And if men and women don't see eye to eye on what is and is not sexual harassment, neither do women among themselves. Maybe this is an extreme example, but it does illustrate the point: Who, among those who read it, can forget *Cosmopolitan* editor Helen Gurley Brown's outrageous op-ed piece in the *Wall Street Journal* only weeks after the Hill-Thomas hearings?

Brown shared her view that while she calls herself a "devout feminist," she also believes that "when a man finds you sexually attractive he is paying you a compliment . . . when he doesn't, that's when you have to worry."

"I know about sexual harassment," she explains in the piece. "When I was working my way through secretarial school in Los Angeles at radio station KHJ, and I came in from school every afternoon, some of the men would be playing a dandy game called 'Scuttle.' Rules: All announcers and engineers who weren't busy would select a secretary, chase her down the halls, through the music library, and back to the announcing booths, catch her, and take her panties off. Once the panties were off, the girl could put them back on again. Nothing wicked ever happened. Depantying was the sole object of the game.

"While all this was going on," she continues, "the girl herself usually shrieked, screamed, flailed, blushed, threatened, and pretended to faint, but to my knowledge no scuttler was ever reported to the front office. *Au contraire*, the girls wore their prettiest panties to work."

Not unexpectedly, *Working Woman* editor Lynn Povich took Brown to task in a letter to the editor of the *Journal* shortly thereafter. "Helen, this is not sexual energy," Povich wrote. "This is sexual harassment."

Most women, Povich said, "do not want men taking their panties off in the office. They don't want men chasing them, cornering them, and touching them, either. They want to do a good job, get paid well, and get ahead, without fear or intimidation.". . .

SEXUAL HARASSMENT IS ABOUT POWER

Sexual harassment isn't about sex. It's about the abuse of power. Sexual discrimination in employment is illegal under Title VII of the Civil Rights Act of 1964. The Equal Employment Opportunity Commission, which enforces the Act, defines sexual harassment as any unwelcome sexual contact that is a term or condition of employment or that creates an intimidating, hostile, or offensive work environment.

The EEOC guidelines also make it clear that the harasser can be a supervisor, co-worker, or even a non-employee (for instance, a client, customer, vendor, or—yes—a source). Often in the case of so-called hostile-environment harassment, the behavior must be repeated over a period of time to qualify as such. However, in the case of "quid pro quo" harassment—where, say, you are promised a promotion only if you sleep with the boss—once is enough.

"Sexual harassment doesn't take place in a vacuum," argue Bravo and Cassedy in *The 9to5 Guide to Combating Sexual Harassment.* "It is the relatively low status of women in the work world that makes the problem so widespread and so persistent. And if harassment stems from women's inferior position on the job, it also functions to keep women there."

This resource of theirs is a must for every working woman's bookshelf. Taking a no-nonsense approach, the authors cover quite a bit of ground, from focusing on what sexual harassment is and isn't and countering the myths about it, to providing specific advice as to what action you should take if you think it is happening to you. That includes making it clear to the harasser, either in person or in writing, that the behavior is unwanted; documenting the incidents as well as your own job performance, and letting a third party know that the problem exists. (In investigating claims, EEOC attorneys have said they generally look first to see if these steps were taken.)

Most importantly, "Trust your instincts," the 9to5 book advises. "When social workers teach children about sexual assault and unwanted touching, they talk about the 'uh-oh' feeling. . . . If the 'uh-oh' feeling gets triggered, don't ignore it."

THE FICTION OF THE "STERILE" WORKPLACE

While attorneys William Petrocelli and Barbara Kate Repa argue in *Sexual Harassment on the Job* that the "impending peril of the sterile workplace is greatly exaggerated," and that male agonizing "should result in more would-be harassers reining in their obnoxious workplace behavior," they admit there may also be a downside.

They suggest that "excessive male hand-wringing over what is and what is not acceptable behavior may once again be engineered to make women feel foolish and intimidated—to still their tongues about harassment."

Even though the number of sexual-harassment claims filed with the EEOC has risen dramatically since the Hill-Thomas hearings, many women are still afraid to speak up. This really shouldn't come as a surprise. A columnist for the *Star-Ledger* newspaper in New Jersey wrote shortly after the hearings that "in the workplace there are people, women and men, who do not feel able to burn any 'bridges,' who feel the need to compromise and maintain the contact, to swallow an insult or live with indignities in order to accomplish their career goals, or to just keep their job."

The fear of humiliation is another factor. "Reporting sexual harassment can mean describing offensive events repeatedly, in detail, in the presence of company officials, lawyers, agency staff, court personnel—and the harasser himself," the 9to5 authors argue in their book. "All too often, the victim's behavior, not the harasser's, becomes the issue."

Take a moment to think back on what Anita Hill endured at the hands of that all-male Senate Judiciary Committee. Never mind that she was Clarence Thomas's accuser; she ended up being the one on trial. . . .

A Safer Workplace

It's ironic, at a time when sexual harassment is talked about more freely than ever, that many courageous women who do decide to speak up about their experiences often find themselves ultimately silenced by gag orders imposed as part of settlement agreements they reach with their alleged harassers and/or employers.

It's too bad, really, because resorting to such measures only serves to sweep the issue under the carpet instead of keeping it out in the open. I suppose this suits many of the harassers and their employers, but it does little to further public awareness of the issue and, more importantly, efforts to stop it.

"Making the workplace a safer, more productive place for ourselves and our daughters should be on the agenda for each of us," says Anita Hill, in a speech reprinted in *Sexual Harassment: Know Your Rights!*

"It is something we can do for ourselves."

| "Today's businesswomen are being taught that behavior they once would have considered boorish or inappropriate constitutes actionable sexual harassment."

THE PROBLEM OF SEXUAL HARASSMENT HAS BEEN EXAGGERATED

Elizabeth Larson

Elizabeth Larson has written on women's business issues for *Investor's Business Daily*, the *American Enterprise*, the Knight-Ridder Financial News Service, and the *Women's Quarterly*, a conservative women's journal. In the following viewpoint, Larson contends that in the wake of Anita Hill's 1991 charges of sexual harassment against Supreme Court nominee Clarence Thomas, the problem of sexual harassment in the workplace has been exaggerated. Attempts by corporations to educate employees about sexual harassment have instead encouraged women to file baseless sexual harassment claims, she argues. Larson concludes that this increase in sexual harassment lawsuits has created a false impression that harassment is rampant in corporate America.

As you read, consider the following questions:

1. By how much did the number of sexual harassment cases increase between 1991 and 1993, according to Larson?
2. How was the case of *Barnes v. Train* resolved, according to the author?
3. What backlash does Larson predict in response to the increase in sexual harassment accusations?

A re American men becoming sexual predators on a scale unimaginable even to Anita Hill? The proposition that thousands of male bosses are lurching across their desks at their female underlings may surprise many working women in these sexually frosty times. Yet that's exactly what the statistics seem to show.

More Sexual Harassment Cases

Since Hill made her accusations against Clarence Thomas in 1991, the number of sexual harassment charges filed with the Equal Employment Opportunity Commission has more than doubled: from 6,127 cases in 1990 to 14,420 in 1994. (The EEOC saw a twenty-three percent surge in complaints in the first three weeks following the hearings.) Even before Anita Hill, the number of complaints filed with the EEOC had been steadily rising, from just 3,661 cases in 1981.

In response to this alarming trend, American corporations are spending thousands of dollars on seminars to educate their employees about sexual harassment and in-house officers to deal with complaints before they get filed. The truth, though, is that these armies of experts may be fueling the problem rather than containing it. Like the college students persuaded by their feminist sisters that an unwanted kiss is really rape, today's businesswomen are being taught that behavior they once would have considered boorish or inappropriate constitutes actionable sexual harassment. Employers may think they are hiring consultants to protect them from lawsuits, but what is actually being taught is a very different lesson: a wink or a leer can be money in the bank.

The lesson is being learned: The frequency of lawsuits and the size of settlements being awarded seem only to increase as the gravity of the complaints shrink. Thus the real explanation for the EEOC's eye-popping statistics may be less due to lascivious bosses than to a growing number of women, many spurred on by Anita Hill's example, who find it more profitable to litigate than to work.

The First Case

Brace yourself for the facts of what is believed to be the first sexual harassment case, *Barnes v. Train*, in 1974. A woman working at the Environmental Protection Agency alleged that her job was abolished after she refused to engage in an affair with her boss. A federal district court dismissed the case because, although it agreed that Barnes had suffered discrimination, this discrimination was based not on the fact that she was a woman, but on her refusal to have sex with the director of the agency. For that, the district court said, the law offered no remedy. The decision was reversed on appeal, and Barnes was eventually awarded $18,000 in back pay as damages.

Move forward twenty-one years. Wal-Mart is now appealing a 1995 court ruling that awarded $50 million in punitive damages to a worker in its receiving department who charged that her supervisor liked to joke about her figure.

How did this happen? How did the courts come to regard a tasteless remark as nearly three thousand times more serious than a woman losing her job for refusing sex with her boss?

WORKPLACE TENSIONS

The current approach to sexual harassment has clearly hurt working relationships between men and women. Men are retreating to the safety of their offices, avoiding private contact with female co-workers, and carefully censoring their speech. . . .

Most of the outcry over sexual harassment is not about bosses demanding sex but about men doing and saying things that some women find offensive. Perhaps women are behaving just as offensively, but men have learned to live with it. The real answer to the "hostile environment" problem may be that women should learn to live with it too.

Harsh Luthar and Anthony Townsend, *National Review*, February 6, 1995.

Like the concept of "date rape," the term "sexual harassment" didn't even exist two decades ago. It joined the American lexicon in the late 1970s with the publication of Lin Farley's *Sexual Shakedown: The Sexual Harassment of Women on the Job* (1978) and Catharine MacKinnon's *Sexual Harassment of Working Women* (1979). MacKinnon, the well-known feminist law professor, was largely responsible for convincing the legal community that sexual harassment is a form of sex discrimination. In the 1986 case *Meritor Savings Bank v. Vinson*, the court upheld MacKinnon's "hostile environment" argument for the first time. This dramatically increased an employer's potential liability because the plaintiff was no longer required to prove she had been subject to a threat (*e.g.*, "Have sex with me or you're fired")—only that she found herself uncomfortable at work, whether because of male comments (*e.g.*, "Nice blouse you have on") or—as in the *Jacksonville Shipyards* case—because of sexy pinups on the wall. As libertarian professor Ellen Frankel Paul has noted, our legal system has gone from punishing behavior that is objectively wrong to that which is subjectively offensive. As the courts' sympathy towards acutely sensitive women has expanded, the average amount awarded in sexual harassment cases has multiplied to some $250,000 today, according to the trade journal *Business Insurance*.

THE COST TO BUSINESSES

While relatively few women filing complaints actually get a shot at this legal jackpot (the EEOC ended up litigating only fifty cases in 1990), the cost to businesses attempting to avoid harassment charges is huge. Sexual harassment seminars run by professional consultants and legal advisors range in length from four hours to two days and can cost several thousand dollars each time. And that's just the beginning. As the *9to5 Guide to Combatting Sexual Harassment* suggests, "Training should be ongoing, not a onetime session, and presented on paid time." Another guide for employers, *Sexual Harassment on the Job*, recommends that companies have their employees complete a "Sexual Harassment Survey" every six months. And don't forget that every new employee—especially those in management—should go through an awareness and prevention program if the company is to minimize its risk.

In some areas of the country, these voluntary efforts are required by law. Since 1993, California has required all companies, regardless of size, to notify their employees that sexual harassment is unlawful. The employer must provide examples of what constitutes sexual harassment and make sure it has explained how employees can get in touch with government agencies to deal with their complaints. Connecticut companies with more than fifty workers have been required since 1991 to conduct at least two hours of sexual harassment awareness training for all management; in any office with more than three workers, posters about sexual harassment must be prominently displayed.

No wonder that companies are now purchasing "sexual harassment liability insurance." Invented in the aftermath of the Clarence Thomas hearings, premiums for this insurance range from $1,500 to $25,000 annually, depending on various factors, including whether a company has faced harassment charges before. Although fewer than half of the Fortune 500 companies currently have sexual harassment coverage, insurance company officials predict it will become a standard part of most business insurance portfolios over the next few years.

Such coverage would have helped someone like Bill Buckingham, president of Buckingham Computer Services Inc., who fired a woman for incompetence. "I'll get even" were the last words he heard from his disgruntled employee as she left his office. She sued Buckingham and his company, a computer consulting business with some forty employees, for sexual harassment and wrongful discharge.

"Her comment was that I touched her on the back, which I had," Buckingham told reporters. "We're a pretty close-knit company, and there was no question that I had patted people on the back. Nothing sexual. I'd tell people that they were looking sharp today, ask if that was a new dress, stuff like that."

His former employee demanded more than $100,000 to settle the case. Since that figure represented a year's profits, Buckingham tried to fight. He gave up in 1992 after an eighteen-month battle and $25,000 in legal costs.

PUNISHING WORKING WOMEN

You could say that the rapid growth of the sexual harassment industry is liberalism's tax on business. The culture of victimization is becoming so embedded in the courts and legislatures that a handful of sexual harassment lawsuits are now seen as representative of the average working woman's lot. Rather than limiting themselves to explanations of the law, experts are teaching women to spot lechery behind every friendly smile. In a sense, this teaching is perhaps a response to that other outcome of sixties' liberalism: the degradation of manners and codes of social behavior. Without clear rules of etiquette, it's no wonder men and women alike need workplace manuals to know how to behave—manuals that unfortunately encourage women to run to the courts at every little slight, real or imagined.

Yet this zeal to punish employers will also punish working women. If women are going to continue to make inroads into the workforce, they will have to deal with office cranks and curmudgeons, louts and Lotharios, backstabbers and boors—just as men have always had to do. It's hard to legislate away unpleasant personalities. In the end, the true backlash against women will not stem from lewd, sexist male bosses but from something far more threatening to the achievements of women: an employer's silent rejection of a woman's job application for fear of trouble.

"Military life may have unique
features that make a sexually mixed
culture especially difficult to
sustain."

THE INTEGRATION OF WOMEN HAS CAUSED SEXUAL HARASSMENT IN THE MILITARY

Maggie Gallagher

Integrating military women into formerly all-male units has resulted in sexual harassment and other types of sexual misconduct, asserts Maggie Gallagher in the following viewpoint. Military women, she contends, are uniquely vulnerable to sexual
abuse because they are under the direct command of male superior officers, they cannot quit if harassed, and they are trained to
follow orders. Gallagher concludes that efforts to further integrate the armed forces harm both women and the military. Gallagher is a syndicated columnist and the author of *The Abolition of
Marriage: How We Destroy Lasting Love*.

As you read, consider the following questions:

1. According to Gallagher, how many military women reported
   being sexually harassed in 1996?
2. How does Gallagher respond to critics who suggest that
   women should be put in combat positions?

From Maggie Gallagher, "Military Experience in Battle of the Sexes," *Washington Times*,
February 19, 1997. Reprinted by permission of the *Washington Times*.

M ilitary sex scandals seem to have taken on an eerily time-less quality: In 1980, for example, half of 300 Army women stationed in Germany said they had been subjected to unwanted physical advances; in 1988, a majority of military women said they encountered some form of sexual harassment. In 1996, it was 55 percent.

THE PROBLEM WITH INTEGRATING WOMEN

These seemingly perpetual troubles integrating women into the armed forces stand in marked contrast to the military's success with race, a testament to which can be found in the sight of one high-ranking black man, Secretary of the Army Togo D. West Jr., on television defending the rights of another high-ranking black man, Army Sgt. Maj. Gene McKinney, against a white sergeant major's charge that he kissed her in a military hotel room.

The relative difficulty the military has had integrating the sexes, as compared to races, is of course exactly the opposite of the civilian experience, where colleges and corporations alike more easily absorbed larger numbers of women than minorities.

Military life may have unique features that make a sexually mixed culture especially difficult to sustain. For example, it is actually illegal for women soldiers to quit, which reduces their ability to resist sexual exploitation in the first place, or to report it afterward. And don't forget to factor in the strange power of persuasion a military superior can exercise over a soldier trained to obey orders.

Consider the case of poor Jessica Bleckley, an 18-year-old Army recruit, who told the *New York Times* a drill sergeant ordered her to have sex with him. According to Jessica, it wasn't rape; she just assumed she had to obey.

A few months later, after she lodged a complaint, Ms. Bleckley accidentally ran into the drill sergeant. Once again, he ordered her to lie down on the floor of a nearby office latrine and have sex, and once again, she felt bound to comply.

This is not the kind of thing that has any easy civilian analog. In private life, a boss who wanted such crude sexual favors from an employee would undoubtedly have to at least hint at repercussions or imply favors. Only in the military, one suspects, would a simple voice command produce the desired results.

COMBAT AND SEXUAL HARASSMENT

Civilian advocates of a unisex military have their own answer for why sexual harassment seems so hard to root out of military life. Senator Olympia Snowe, Maine Republican, blamed women's continued exclusion from combat, arguing, "Every time a woman is excluded from a position, she's devalued." Just put women in the trenches and men will no longer seek inappropriate sexual contact.

Uh, right.

A NUTTY NATIONAL POLICY

Senior officers, terrified of speaking the truth in public, know that for political reasons we're indulging in a nutty national policy of throwing healthy young men and women together in adversarial hierarchical positions, training them for battle with no concern for the consequences of the real world.

"We can get away with only frequent episodes of embarrassment as long as we don't have to fight a war," says one of these senior officers. "But a catastrophe of the kind we've never had before is inevitable, and everyone from the commander-in-chief down knows it."

Suzanne Fields, *Washington Times*, November 18, 1996.

Enlisted women certainly don't see it Mrs. Snowe's way: Sixty-one percent say sexual harassment would increase if women were sent into combat. Just 3 percent of enlisted women agree they "should be treated exactly like men and serve in the combat arms just like men."

How can a woman who requires the assistance of the law to cope with a supervisor's kiss be expected to deal with a bayonet thrust?

THE EFFECT ON THE MILITARY

"The time has finally come," writes former Navy Secretary James Webb in the *Weekly Standard*, "to cease examining these issues solely from the perspective of how military culture should adjust itself for women." The Army, Navy, Air Force and Marines do not exist to provide equal opportunity for anybody. On all the gender issues, from women in combat to ending unisex training, the only real question should be: Does this policy help or hurt the military's role in defending American liberty?

For when push comes to shove, what's good for the Army is what's good for American women, and not the other way around.

"For a young woman to be sexually assaulted by her drill sergeant is like being molested by her father."

THE INTEGRATION OF WOMEN IS NOT THE CAUSE OF SEXUAL HARASSMENT IN THE MILITARY

Harry Summers Jr.

Harry Summers Jr. is a distinguished fellow at the Army War College. In the following viewpoint, Summers agrees that military women are more vulnerable to sexual harassment and rape because they are often under the direct command of male superior officers. However, he rejects the contention that such behavior is an inevitable consequence of attempts to integrate women into the armed forces. Summers concludes that a climate of lax discipline, not simply the presence of women, is ultimately responsible for the pervasiveness of sexual abuse in the military.

As you read, consider the following questions:

1. Why was the Tailhook scandal less serious than the events at the Aberdeen Proving Grounds, according to Summers?
2. According to the author, what is fundamental to being a leader?

From Harry Summers Jr., "Army Scandal Claims Trust as a Casualty," *Los Angeles Times*, editorial, November 12, 1996. Reprinted by permission of the author.

"**Y**our drill sergeants are kind of like your family," said a female trainee at the Ordnance School at the Army's Aberdeen Proving Grounds in Maryland. "You really don't expect them to do such terrible things to you." Her remarks revealed why the sex scandal unfolding there is so heinous, and why the Army leadership is responding with anger and concern.

The 1991 Tailhook scandal involved Navy female officers and civilian women who were there of their own free will. Their molestation, while reprehensible, does not compare with the near incestuous incidents at Aberdeen, where male drill sergeants allegedly preyed on women in their charge. "What is being alleged here is a basic violation of trust, an abuse of authority," said Army Chief of Staff Gen. Dennis Reimer. That strikes at the heart of the Army's being.

TRUST IS A PREREQUISITE

Trust is one of the prerequisites specifically spelled out in an officer's commission and is implicit in the warrant of a noncommissioned officer as well. That's because success on the battlefield requires you to literally trust your leaders with your life.

Building trust, especially in sergeants, is what basic training and advanced military training are all about. Thus, for a young woman to be sexually assaulted by her drill sergeant is like being molested by her father. The damage is not only to her, but to the Army's entire command climate.

The incidents at Aberdeen were disturbing enough, but equally troubling were the reactions of the female trainees there.

"They were not surprised by the charges," reported the *Washington Post*. "They described a gossipy atmosphere . . . in which rumors of fraternization and allegations of sexual harassment loom large." Disturbing as well were the excuses given, ironically enough, by other female trainees. "I think females are throwing themselves at the drill sergeants," said one. Others agreed that many of the incidents were "consensual."

But as the Aberdeen commander, Maj. Gen. Robert D. Shadley, said, those excuses won't wash. Because of the authority an instructor wields, "there is no such thing as consensual sex between a superior and a trainee."

More despicable were those who blamed the incidents on attempts to "feminize" the Army. Retired Army lawyer Col. Dick Black told the *Washington Times* that "the heart of the whole problem is mixed-gender training." Sexual liaisons between drill sergeants and their trainees "is as predictable as human nature. Think of yourself when you were 25. Wouldn't you love to have a group of 19-year-old girls under your control day in, day out?"

In the military, self-control is fundamental to being a leader. As Shadley commented, we want "leaders, not lechers." Dismissing the "feminization" issue, Army Secretary Togo West said such arguments "disregard the nature of our society and our responsibility. There is no segregation . . . in the defense of our country."

U.S. Army target practice.

Paul Conrad, ©1996, Los Angeles Times. Reprinted with permission.

There is no doubt, however, that the drill sergeant-trainee relationship creates enormous opportunities for corruption. A 19-year-old infantry sergeant fresh from the Korean War battlefield, I was assigned to the Ordnance Replacement Training Center at Aberdeen in 1951 as a drill sergeant. It was the nearest to being God that I have ever been. My recruits, all male, were draftees in their late 20s or early 30s. Even though they were much older and wiser, a harsh glance from me would have them literally trembling in their boots. Fortunately, the command climate then tolerated no abuses.

The rules to prevent such corruption have been there for years. Evidently vigilance in their enforcement has not. A crackdown on discipline and a reemphasis on leadership are imperative. To its credit, the Army's chain-of-command is responding.

PERIODICAL BIBLIOGRAPHY

The following articles have been selected to supplement the diverse views presented in this chapter. Addresses are provided for periodicals not indexed in the *Readers' Guide to Periodical Literature*, the *Alternative Press Index*, the *Social Sciences Index*, or the *Index to Legal Periodicals and Books*.

Kathryn Abrams	"The Reasonable Woman," *Dissent*, Winter 1995.
Alexandra Alger and William G. Flanagan	"Sexual Politics," *Forbes*, May 6, 1996.
Mona Charen	"Feminists Are Losing the Battle," *Conservative Chronicle*, April 13, 1994. Available from PO Box 29, Hampton, IA 50441.
Alba Conte	"When the Tables Are Turned," *Trial*, March 1996.
Tamina Davar	"Indecent Proposals," *A. Magazine*, October/November 1996. Available from 270 Lafayette St., Suite 400, New York, NY 10012.
Suzanne Fields	"Battle of the Sexes Drifts into Dangerous Territory," *Insight*, July 5, 1993. Available from 3600 New York Ave. NE, Washington, DC 20002.
William Norman Grigg	"A New Tool for Feminists," *New American*, July 26, 1993. Available from PO Box 8040, Appleton, WI 54913.
Kristin Downey Grimsley	"Confronting Hard-Core Harassers," *Washington Post*, January 27, 1997. Available from PO Box 1150 15th St. NW, Washington, DC 20071.
Jane Gross	"Now Look Who's Taunting: Now Look Who's Suing," *New York Times*, February 26, 1995.
Dianne Hales	"Sex in the Workplace," *Reader's Digest*, February 1996.
Peter T. Kilborn	"Sex Abuse Cases Stun Pentagon, but the Problem Has Deep Roots," *New York Times*, February 10, 1997.
Elizabeth Larson	"The Economic Costs of Sexual Harassment," *Freeman*, August 1996. Available from Foundation for Economic Education, 30 S. Broadway, Irvington, NY 10533.

Harsh Luthar and Anthony Townsend	"Man Handling," *National Review*, February 6, 1995.
Wendy McElroy	"Sexual Harassment: What Is It?" *Freeman*, June 1993.
William Murchison	"Spit Polish, Nail Polish Don't Mix," *Conservative Chronicle*, December 4, 1996.
Sharon Nelton	"Sexual Harassment; Reducing the Risks," *Nation's Business*, March 1995.
Li Onesto	"Rape in Uniform," *Revolutionary Worker*, December 15, 1996. Available from RCP Publications, PO Box 3486, Merchandise Mart, Chicago, IL 60654.
Dana Priest	"Aberdeen and Tailhook: Like Apples and Oranges," *Washington Post National Weekly Edition*, March 31, 1997.
Carl Rowan	"Sex in the Military," *Liberal Opinion*, April 10, 1997. Available from PO Box 468, Vinton, IA 52349.
Margot Slade	"Sexual Harassment: Stories from the Field," *New York Times*, March 27, 1994.
Kara Swisher	"Corporations Are Seeing the Light on Harassment," *Washington Post National Weekly Edition*, February 14–20, 1994.
Tim Wheeler	"Rape, Harassment Scandal Rocks U.S. Army," *People's Weekly World*, November 16, 1996. Available from 235 W. 23rd St., New York, NY 10011.

CHAPTER 4

SHOULD WOMEN SERVE IN THE MILITARY?

CHAPTER PREFACE

American women have always participated in the nation's defense. During the Revolutionary and Civil Wars, a small number of women disguised themselves as men in order to enlist and fight. More often, women served as nurses, but they did so as citizens employed by the military rather than as enlisted personnel. At the turn of the twentieth century, the army and the navy established auxiliary Nurse Corps. The Nurse Corps were officially recognized as being part of the military, but the nurses were not given military ranks or benefits.

The navy and the marines first enlisted women in World War I, primarily as clerical workers but also as translators, recruiters, radio technicians, and telephone operators. This measure was seen as a wartime expedience, and the women were demobilized after the war. During World War II, women were recruited for new, temporary military organizations: the Women's Army Corps (WAC), the Navy Women's Reserve (called WAVES), and the Marine Corps Women's Reserve. Again, most of the women in these corps held clerical support positions, but some served in such capacities as control tower operators, mechanics, navigation instructors, and pilots.

When World War II ended, the U.S. military requested that the women's corps be made permanent. On June 12, 1948, President Harry Truman signed the Women's Armed Service Act, which gave permanent military status to these corps—including the newly formed Women in the Air Force (WAF)—and allowed women to enlist during peacetime. However, the act placed a number of restrictions on female soldiers. For example, it limited servicewomen to no more than 2 percent of the total military and set a cap on the number of female officers. The law also barred women from combat positions.

Many of these restrictions were removed in the 1960s and 1970s. By the end of the 1970s, the ceilings on promotions and on the total number of female soldiers had been rescinded and the separate women's corps had been abolished, resulting in the integration of some previously all-male units. The combat ban held until after the 1991 Persian Gulf War. Approximately 40,000 American female soldiers took part in that war, many in hazardous occupations and some near the front lines. Shortly after the war, U.S. military and political leaders began to reconsider the combat exclusion rule.

In 1993, then–Defense Secretary Les Aspin ordered the armed forces to allow women on surface warships and combat aircraft and to present justification for barring women from other combat positions. In response, the four branches of the military began to integrate women into some combat roles and to assess the feasibility of opening other combat positions to female soldiers.

As of 1997, submarines and most ground combat assignments—including armory, infantry, and field artillery units—remained off-limits to women. On the other hand, women had begun to fly combat planes and to serve on warships.

This opening of roles to servicewomen, as well as the possibility of further expansion in the near future, has ignited much controversy. Many commentators believe that female soldiers should not be allowed to take part in combat. They argue that women are physically incapable of participating in certain types of warfare, especially ground combat. According to syndicated columnist Charles Reese, "Differences in physical strength, heart-lung capacity, hormones and bone structure . . . make women unsuitable for combat." Allowing women to participate in combat despite these physical differences will lower America's military readiness, opponents maintain. Phyllis Schlafly, an advocate of traditional gender roles and family values, is among those who question the wisdom of making "personnel policy decisions about women on the basis of 'equal rights' and 'career opportunity' rather than military need and readiness."

Other commentators counter that women are capable of filling most or all combat roles, especially as warfare becomes increasingly mechanized or computerized. Edward N. Luttwak, a military consultant and senior fellow at the Center for Strategic and International Studies, claims: "In a nuclear submarine all the jobs could be done by women with their left hand." Furthermore, many servicewomen and others point out that advancement in the military usually hinges on experience in combat units. Rules barring women from such units hurt the military, they maintain, because the most qualified women often are not utilized to their utmost ability.

As the number of women joining the U.S. military continues to grow, the controversy over their role is also likely to increase. The following chapter presents various debates on women's participation in the military.

"There is no perceptible difference
between men and women in
performance and war-fighting
spirit."

SEXUAL INTEGRATION HAS NOT HARMED THE MILITARY

Dana Priest

Dana Priest is a staff writer for the *Washington Post*, a daily newspaper based in Washington, D.C. In 1997, Priest visited a sexually integrated U.S. military police battalion that was part of an
international peacekeeping operation in Bosnia and reported on
the interactions between the male and female soldiers. According to the author, for the most part the men and women in the
battalion have served together effectively, readily adapting to
shared living quarters with minimal occurrences of sexual misconduct. Furthermore, Priest writes, the women have proven
themselves to be tough and competent soldiers and have won
the respect of their male colleagues.

As you read, consider the following questions:

1. What is the most important quality to instill in female
   soldiers, according to Mary C. Frels, as quoted by the author?
2. Why do team members prefer to share the same field tent,
   according to Priest?
3. According to Michael Thompson, as cited by the author, why
   did he initially not realize that some of the military police
   guarding his convoy were women?

From Dana Priest, "Engendering a Warrior Spirit," *Washington Post*, March 10, 1997.
Copyright ©1997, The Washington Post. Reprinted with permission.

S pec. Claudia Colburn gets so excited she leaps from her seat in the crowded mess hall here [in Camp Demi, Bosnia]. Spreading her feet apart as her squad members move aside, she takes hold of an imaginary weapon and pretends to spray the room with rounds.

"I love firing the M-19, you get a hype," she says of the Mark-19 grenade launcher, which sits beside her every day atop a U.S. Army armored vehicle rumbling over hilly Bosnian roads. "But we've been here for seven months, and we haven't gotten to fire. It's like a buildup of frustration."

Moments later Colburn gets even more excited as she talks of the time local Serbs let her fire one of their AK-47 automatic rifles on a practice range. She lets out a primal, guttural yell: "Ahhh!"

The frustration is gone.

Spec. Christopher Santiago, a member of Colburn's squad, laughs and shakes his head: "Spec. Colburn, she's one of the best."

WOMEN AS WARRIORS

For all the recent publicity over problems between men and women in military bases back home, relations between the sexes here in the field are easygoing and untroubled, judging from a week spent with U.S. peacekeeping troops in Bosnia.

There is no perceptible difference between men and women in performance and war-fighting spirit, and, if anything, the women are as stereotypically macho as their male counterparts.

"The most important thing is to instill the warrior spirit," says Lt. Col. Mary C. Frels, commander of the 720th Military Police Battalion in which Colburn and Santiago serve. "If a woman thinks like a warrior, believes she's a warrior, then she'll do what it takes. Most women don't think they have it in them, but once you let that spirit loose you find that aggressiveness."

Asked in dozens of interviews about the changes that have had to be made for women in military police (MP) squads, soldiers and officers are uniformly nonchalant about what they describe as routine adjustments. Most often, they responded with down-to-earth examples about going to the bathroom in the field and pulling up rain ponchos for privacy in the tents they share.

"What's the big deal?" says Sgt. Steven Davis, 27, who has women in his squad. "We're not sleeping together, we're just sleeping together."

Some members of Congress have argued that Army problems with sexual misconduct show that integrating women into the armed forces does not—and will never—work well. At the heart of that concern are beliefs that individuals' sex drives will overwhelm good order and discipline, and that women are not inherently the kind of warriors men have been throughout history.

"There's a natural tension, I think, a sexual tension, that exists between male and female in almost every sphere of human activity," Republican Senator Dan Coats of Indiana said at a recent congressional hearing. "I find it hard to believe that we can ever create an atmosphere, particularly in the military, where we don't add to this tension rather than reduce this tension."

REALITY IN THE FIELD

That is not the reality on the ground for the troops of the 720th MP Battalion.

Here it is often impossible to tell the women from the men. To reduce the risk to U.S. troops, soldiers are ordered to wear bulky flak jackets and helmets and to carry their weapons at all times. (They get to take off their helmets at meals.)

Some of the best gunners—the ones with the biggest, heaviest firepower—are women who ride in the open hatches of the muddy, olive drab armored convoys that bump around Bosnia every day. If not for their higher pitch of voice, it would be hard to tell by words alone whether a man or a woman is the one yelling or cussing.

KEEPING THE FIGHTING SPIRIT

The most amorphous rap against women in the service—and the hardest to disprove—is that they will weaken the warrior culture, the fighting spirit and tight bonding of buddies in the trenches. Such fears were not borne out by the gulf war, where 40,000 women served alongside 550,000 men. Integrated units seemed to perform as well as all-male units. There was plenty of sex—except in the 24th Mechanized Division, whose commander, Gen. Barry McCaffrey, decreed that "soldiers don't dance with other soldiers." Teamwork overcame physical differences. After-action surveys found that as units got closer to combat, they began to forget about male-female differences.

John Barry and Evan Thomas, *Newsweek*, May 12, 1997.

Sexual misconduct is something soldiers here have read about in the *Stars and Stripes* newspaper, and many have been baffled and saddened by reports of rape at Army training centers and of allegations that the sergeant major of the Army, Gene C. McKinney, had harassed several women.

The large number of allegations makes clear that the Army's "zero tolerance" for sexual misconduct is still just a slogan. But Army statistics also show that sexual misconduct is less of a problem when troops are deployed with a purposeful mission than when they are back at their home bases, or in administrative and headquarters units.

SEX AND ROMANCE

There have been seven allegations of sexual misconduct and three of improper consensual relationships among the troops of the 1st Infantry Division that deployed to Bosnia in November 1996.

Some 174 women out of the 4,970 who have been in the overall Bosnia operation since November 1995—including those who worked in logistics bases in Hungary and Croatia—have been sent home early because they were pregnant. That 3.5 percent pregnancy rate is half the Navy's shipboard rate and lower than the 4.3 percent pregnancy rate for Army women who have remained elsewhere in Europe.

That's not to say that romance, or sex, doesn't happen here.

One woman from the 720th has been sent home early from Bosnia. She was a cook who became pregnant two months after her boyfriend was assigned to Camp Demi.

Cpl. Charles Stockwell, 26, is happy to hear his wife's voice over the radio each time his unit passes her checkpoint. But the relationship didn't start here: They were married before they came to Bosnia.

Specs. John Clark and Robin Griggers are engaged and in the same platoon. Although they like being at the same camp, both admit they worry more about each other's safety. "We agreed if we ever got married we'd leave the same platoon," Clark says. They started dating before Bosnia, and everyone at Camp Demi knows they're a couple.

Under Army rules, consensual heterosexual sex is not permitted between enlisted personnel and officers in the same chain of command, or between anyone else if it negatively affects good order and discipline, a judgment left to the discretion of individual commanders. Homosexual sex is prohibited.

MAKING ADJUSTMENTS

In a peacekeeping role like the one here, the duties of the sexually integrated military police place them even closer to what would be considered a front line than the all-male infantry, artillery and armor units.

Troops from the 720th MPs are sent out to talk with local army leaders or to protect other U.S. Army officers who must make sure the Serbs or Muslims are not preparing to fight again, that they warehouse their armaments and that they allow refugees to return safely to their homes.

Women have been a part of the MPs since the mid-1970s. Because of this, troops long ago learned to make necessary adjustments and have been passing them on to new soldiers ever since.

Women get privacy when they have to go to the bathroom in the woods—the two females in one team have conditioned themselves to go at the same time. However, some women have been known to deliberately dehydrate themselves to avoid having to urinate, a practice that the Army discourages for health reasons.

At some camps, such as Camp McGovern and Tuzla, women and men share large tents divided by wooden bookshelves or planks. At others, like Camp Demi, they sleep separately in small two- and six-person trailers.

With few exceptions, team members say they prefer to share the same field tent because it's good for unit morale and cohesion, and besides, then no one misses out on the casual day's-end discussion of the next day's mission. Troops hang a poncho between men's and women's sleeping bags when squads spend the night in field tents together. Or they leave the tent when members of the opposite sex are changing clothes.

"Do You Feel Like a Man?"

If anything, gender is sometimes the butt of relaxed humor. Several weeks ago the humvee drivers at Camp Demi put on a skit about their commanders. Lt. Cecilia Armendariz's driver discussed how having a female commander affected his manhood.

"My lieutenant burps, farts, smokes, scratches, dips and spits more than I do, and she's a female," he said. "I have a hard time with my manhood."

"I have a solution," answered another driver. "Every time you feel your manhood dipping down, take a little bit of this." He then stuffed a huge wad of chewing tobacco, which Armendariz chews, into her driver's cheeks.

"Do you feel like a man?" he yelled. "Do you feel like a man?"

Armendariz is tough, the men say. When she earned her lieutenant's bar in 1996, she asked her company commander, Capt. Zane Jones, to hit it into her collarbone, piercing the flesh with the pin, a long Army tradition. He complied with a punch and without a thought.

"I pulled it out and heard a pop," Armendariz recalls matter-of-factly.

"I had heard about Lt. Armendariz and had done some politicking to get her," says Jones, staring straight into her eyes over coffee one morning. "I think there's a fantasy among some guys that maybe women can't do this. But then they get around them and find out they can."

COMMANDING FEMALE SOLDIERS

Col. Michael Thompson, commander of the Infantry Division's 2nd Brigade, says he was surprised to learn after a week that some of the MPs protecting him in his convoy were women.

"It was winter and we were all bundled up," he says. "I just didn't notice." During that week, he would order the convoy to stop periodically so everyone could stand by the side of the road and relieve themselves. The two women would just turn their heads and wait until they stopped for the day.

Thompson never had commanded women before he came to Bosnia, and when shortly after he arrived a firefight broke out between Russian peacekeeping troops and Serbs, he decided not to take his lawyer, Maj. Sharon Riley, with him to the scene.

WOMEN PROVE THEIR WORTH

Of the 540,000 Americans who served in Operation Desert Storm, nearly 41,000 were women—more than 7 percent of the U.S. forces in the theater. It was the largest wartime deployment of American military women in history. They did just about everything on land, at sea, and in the air except engage in the actual fighting, and even there the line was often a fuzzy one. They piloted and crewed jet planes and helicopters over the battle area, refueled fighters in mid-air, serviced high-tech equipment on the ground, and loaded laser-guided bombs on F-117 Stealths for raids on targets in Baghdad. They directed Patriot missiles, drove trucks, ran enemy prisoner of war facilities, refueled M1 tanks on the side of the road, and guarded bases. They served on naval replenishment and repair ships, fleet oilers, and hospital ships offshore. And in the process many old myths that had hindered their progress in the military were demolished and replaced with surprising new realities.

Jeanne Holm, *Women in the Military*, 1992.

"I was going to a very austere Russian checkpoint with Russian soldiers I didn't know, taking American soldiers into a gunfight to sort things out," he says.

But Riley, who is usually by Thompson's side helping interpret the rules of engagement under the Dayton peace accord, immediately took it as a slight and told her boss, who called Thompson to tell him there were no limitations on what Riley could do. The two laugh about it now.

"There wasn't even a place to take a leak," Thompson says.

"I neglected to tell him I was a Girl Scout and I was used to peeing in the woods," says Riley.

"I've gotten an education on how well they've adapted," Thompson says. "It's not at all new to them."

MAKING CHANGES

And especially not to Lt. Col. Frels, the commander of the 720th. When she joined the Army, women were segregated in training and mission. Now her troops refer to her in conversation simply as "She." A 16-year Army officer, she is one of the only women around who wears any makeup. She's also tough-mouthed, loud and, well, commanding.

Frels also has arranged for bingo on Friday nights—a reaction, she says, to the days she had to go with the guys to beer joints and topless bars if she wanted to socialize with her unit. She recently announced she would start an art fair for local children. Soldiers will be asked to buy their works. And she points out she is probably the first camp commander who has checked the chef's recipes for Thanksgiving and Christmas dinners.

"I cook twice a year," she says. "I just wanted to make sure they got it right."

AN INSPECTION AND A BOUQUET

Her presence has not gone unnoticed outside the camp either.

When Frels first met the Serb lieutenant who controls Srebrenica, a part of the territory she monitors, he was surprised and confused. There are no Serb women in the military. In the middle of her first inspection of a huge weapons storage site that sits across from the former U.N. barracks that was overrun by Serb soldiers in 1995, the lieutenant handed her a bouquet of wildflowers.

Her troops cracked up, and the tension of the moment was broken by their laughter. "I saw on the faces of the other soldiers that this was something unusual," says the Serb lieutenant, who asks not to be identified.

On a recent inspection of the site, Frels meets the lieutenant again. "Did you sexually harass me when you first met me?" she kids with him.

"Who, me?" he responds, grinning.

And then they get down to business. The weapons storage site contains a number of armaments, including AT-4s, an antitank weapon that Frels has the authority to confiscate any time she wants, which is what she reminds him.

"Why would you want to do that?" he asks playfully. "You already have more weapons than you need."

Hands on her hips and a giant smile on her face, she looks up at him and replies, "A woman can never have too many AT-4s."

"We [should not] delude ourselves
into thinking that assimilation of
females into military occupational
specialties is the same as breaching
racial and ethnic barriers."

SEXUAL INTEGRATION HAS HARMED THE MILITARY

James Webb

In the following viewpoint, James Webb contends that the assimilation of women into the U.S. military forces has been problematic. Although Webb concedes that many individual female soldiers have served effectively, he argues that the sexual integration of military units, navy vessels, and basic training camps has led to significant problems with sexual misconduct and harassment. Such problems can cause a dangerous loss of morale among the troops, he maintains. To correct this trend, Webb proposes, the military should return to a policy of segregating male and female soldiers. A veteran of the Vietnam War, Webb served as the assistant secretary of defense and as the secretary of the navy in the Reagan administration.

As you read, consider the following questions:

1. How does Webb describe the military's code of conduct?
2. According to the author, what was the official reason that Commander John Carey was relieved of his command? What was the real reason, in Webb's opinion?
3. In a survey by Laura Miller, cited by the author, how many army women indicated that they would volunteer for combat roles?

Excerpted from James Webb, "The War on the Military Culture," *Weekly Standard*, January 20, 1997. Reprinted by permission of the publisher.

During the summer of 1975, a debate of historic proportions occurred on the floor of the House of Representatives. The debate was significant not because of its rhetoric, which was rather shopworn, or because the issue under discussion was dramatic—a bill mandating the admission of women to the service academies. Rather, the parliamentary methods used by the bill's proponents and their method of argument inaugurated a new era in civil-military relations and have dominated military personnel issues ever since.

The late Sam Stratton of New York, a senior member of the House Armed Services Committee, introduced the measure directly on the House floor as a rider to that year's defense appropriations bill. With the avid assistance of several feminist legislators including Bella Abzug of New York and Pat Schroeder of Colorado, Stratton argued essentially that answering the question of whether women should be permitted to attend the service academies had nothing to do with the manner in which those institutions prepared young men for leadership in combat. Noting that "only" 90 percent of the graduates of those institutions had served in combat-designated billets (the others had been designated "not physically qualified" before graduation), Stratton argued that "the sole issue is a simple matter of equality. . . . All we need is to establish the basic legislative policy that we wish to remove sex discrimination when it comes to admissions to the service academies."

Two New Aspects

The debate added two new dimensions to the way the Congress and other activists would address military issues, particularly those affecting female assimilation. First, Congress took its vote without detailed legislative hearings that would have allowed the military leadership to express its views—a decision that, in effect, told America's military that its perspective was neither respected nor trusted where matters of progressive social policy were concerned.

Second, by focusing the debate on "simple equality" rather than the effect of injecting females into the already complicated and tension-enhancing environment of the operating military, Stratton and company managed to leave a much larger, more intangible, and far more complex issue on the table. And there it has lain ever since.

As a result, no effort has ever really been made to examine the issues raised by the ever-expanding sexual mixing inside the military's unique culture and its requirement of absolute fairness when it comes to administering punishments and rewards. The military is, at its core, a coercive institution, fraught with pressures and unwanted tasks. It relies on a code of conduct that demands egalitarian treatment in every aspect of discipline, recognition, and the subjection of its officers and its ranks to life-threatening risk. When double standards are introduced in matters of physical training and performance, they work against these very criteria.

Furthermore, the sexual jealousies, courtship rituals, and favoritism that are the hallmarks of romantic relationships are inevitable when males and females are brought into close quarters in isolated, intense environments. But these very phenomena inevitably corrode all notions of fairness as the military defines them.

AN ATTACK AGAINST THE MILITARY

These are matters of the utmost seriousness. They are at the center of most of the concerns regarding the assimilation of females into the military. And other than a hapless patchwork of unevenly enforced "fraternization" guidelines, they have never, not once since Sam Stratton's post-Vietnam gambit, been the subject of genuine scrutiny, much less a national debate.

Of course, many of those who voted with Stratton were not only seeking to provide opportunities for women where appropriate to the military's unique mission and operational circumstances, but were actively interested in undoing its historic culture. For those other than the quasi-revolutionaries who took delight in the chaos into which our country had fallen, the summer of 1975 in Washington was a bleak time. Following the embarrassment of our withdrawal from Vietnam, respect for military leadership was at its historic nadir. A year before, President Richard Nixon had resigned in disgrace, and his resignation helped elect the so-called Watergate Congress, 76 Democratic freshmen in the House and eight in the Senate, with a surprising number of activists elected from formerly safe Republican districts. A majority of them had run almost solely on antimilitary and antiwar themes. . . .

Even with the restoration of American respect for the military in the 1980s, the effort to destroy the military culture from the outside has continued unabated, frequently through the use of "wedge" issues involving women. Major changes in female military roles often have been instituted either against the advice of the senior military or without their substantive input. . . .

As these political realities have developed, the military has had to struggle under its own set of unkind realities. Military leaders from their first days in training are steeped in a culture that accepts and believes in civilian control. And they are doers. A policy that was strongly opposed while under consideration will be just as strongly implemented once it is decided upon. Furthermore, generals at the three-star level are selected with (at a minimum) heavy participation from the civilian leadership, and those at the four-star level are chosen at the complete discretion of civilians, allowing politicians to shape the top levels of military leadership. When views on the expansion of female roles become a litmus test for advancement, arguments questioning accepted political wisdom are not conducive to the possibility of reaching the very highest levels.

Mike Shelton/*Orange County Register*. Reprinted with permission.

With little support from the outside, and in a culture that demands performance, those "in the ranks" have learned that pointing out the difficulties inherent in an undertaking as politically volatile as the assimilation of women will quickly end a career. At the same time, enormous pressure is exerted on them to accentuate the positive aspects of this social experiment and ignore or diminish the negative. But male members of the military know that things aren't that simple. As is always true when people are asked to believe in and promote an image they know to be untrue, cynicism soon explodes. This cynicism feeds a backlash, which increases tensions even in areas where women perform well and where their presence is not counterproductive to the military's mission.

These hard realities have created the greatest potential cultural change in our military's history, and if matters are left in this state, we run the risk of destroying all notions of leadership as we have known it. The fundamental disconnect is this: In many areas where females have been introduced into the military, leaders imbued with the imperative of ethical conduct are constantly challenged to hold back on the truth or risk their futures.

ONE SIDE OF THE STORY

And so politicians and media commentators usually end up arguing over only half the story. They are right to call for investigations of commanders who have not dealt preemptively with sexual harassment and unpermitted sex among members of their command. Women forced into unwilling sexual conduct are put into an inexcusable hell when their superior is the culprit, and there is no one to whom they feel they can report the crime.

But politicians and the media are blaming the wrong social forces for such problems. They have not been able to hear from those who have firsthand knowledge of what the sexual integration of the military has meant in matters of military conduct. Consider the commander who knows that the culprit in such situations is not one or a half-dozen individuals, but a system that throws healthy young men and women together inside a volatile, isolated crucible of emotions—a ship at sea or basic training, to take two notable examples. Whom does this commander tell if he believes that the experiment itself has not worked, that the compressed and emotional environment in which these young men and women have been thrust together by unknowing or uncaring policymakers actually encourages disruptive sexual activity?

The commander knows the political mantra since the 1970s has been that sexual misconduct is simply one more cultural problem, and that, like racial insensitivity, it can be overcome by a few lectures and command supervision. He knows also that this is wrong. But to speak his mind or force the issue would most likely be his undoing.

PRESSURE TO IGNORE PROBLEMS

A case in point is Commander John Carey, who took command of the destroyer *Curtis Wilbur* after a fast-track start to his naval career. Soon after, Carey observed two female crew members kissing and spoke to the ship's command chief petty officer of his concern about the disruption such behavior would cause. "Captain," the master chief replied, according to the *Washingtonian*, "there's f——ing going on on this ship 24 hours a day, and there's nothing you can do about it." Carey tried to do something about it and was soon relieved of command for "physically and verbally abusing his crew."

This not-so-subtle pressure to look the other way unless conduct is overt and decidedly nonconsensual permeates civilian policy toward the military. In February 1988, shortly before I resigned as secretary of the Navy, I returned from a trip to U.S. military facilities on Iceland. During a staff meeting with secretary of defense Frank Carlucci, I reported that I had been informed that 51 percent of the single enlisted Air Force females and 48 percent of the single enlisted Navy females stationed in Iceland were pregnant.

Carlucci, who had announced in the first weeks of his tenure that he wished to remove the Reagan administration's policy of restricting women from combat, was unconcerned. "What else is there to do on Iceland?" he replied, drawing titillated chuckles from several sycophantic male military officers at the table. Needless to say, there was no follow-up on this or any other systemic failure, and the uniformed military was given the word through the grapevine that passes from Pentagon aide to general's aide and on down the line that, no matter what written policies might have existed, the leadership was not concerned about sexual fraternization.

The question becomes: Does it matter? And the answer is: In the military, it does.

THE IMPORTANCE OF FAIRNESS

It is difficult to explain to those who have not served in the operational military, and even to many military females who do not comprehend the ethos of units in which women do not serve, why the military is, and must remain, different from the civilian world when it comes to these issues. Next to the clergy, the military is the most values-driven culture in our society. I am not speaking of individual morals; many superb soldiers have been known as "liberty risks" when they are not on duty. Rather, it relates to an impeccable group ethos. Those who serve together must behave toward one another according to a set of unassailable and equally enforced standards—honesty, accountability, sacrifice, and absolute fairness in risk, promotions, and rewards.

The military is, in this sense, a socialist meritocracy. It functions not on money but on nonmaterial recognition. Do something good and you receive a good fitness report, an award, a meritorious mast, promotion to higher rank. Do something bad and you are reprimanded, court-martialed, jailed, demoted. You cannot quit your duties if you don't like your job or your boss or the place they're sending you. Even more astounding, you might be asked to die on behalf of a person or a policy you don't even like. In this environment, fairness is not only crucial, it is the coin of the realm. Fairness is the guarantee that puts credibility into rank, awards, and recognition. And such recognition determines a person's future.

THE DIFFERENCE BETWEEN RACIAL AND SEXUAL INTEGRATION

The military was the first federal institution to create a truly level playing field for minorities. I grew up as the son of a career military officer in the newly integrated military, and I saw it work even through the difficult period of the late 1960s and early 1970s when I was a serving officer of Marines.

Now, to the extent that it is workable, the military has an obligation to provide the same gateways for females, and we should not lose sight either of the talent that many females bring to our armed forces or the wide array of federal benefits that are accorded them for their service in appropriate roles.

But neither should we delude ourselves into thinking that assimilation of females into military occupational specialties is the same as breaching racial and ethnic barriers. Eliminating cultural bias requires intellectual conditioning to break down old attitudes. But eliminating or neutralizing an attraction to the opposite sex requires much sterner and more imaginative therapy, and is probably impossible.

But that is exactly what will have to happen if the military is to work without disruption in the operating units where "group cohesion" is the key to performance, not to mention in the isolated environments of long-term deployments or basic training.

THE RISK OF FAVORITISM

In these circumstances, it is essential that favoritism of all types be minimized and eliminated. But we all know there is no greater or more natural bias than that of an individual toward a beloved. And few emotions are more powerful, or more distracting, than those surrounding the pursuit of, competition for, or the breaking off of amorous relations. In the administration of discipline, benefits, and life-threatening risk, it takes an unusually strong personality to set aside passionate feelings in order to deny a spouse or lover a much-desired benefit or to expose that person to great risk. Nor is it possible to decide an issue in favor of a spouse or lover without at least appearing to be judging matters unfairly.

And there is another problem. Consider a ship on a long sea deployment of perhaps 100 days without a port call, a common enough event in our Navy's recent history. Assume, as is likely, that some members of a mixed crew begin sexual relationships while at sea. What of the rest? They will not have the opportunity to find a partner for months. The inescapable feelings of resentment, competition, or anger that follow create a powder keg of emotions that cannot help but affect morale, discipline, and attention to duty.

No edict from above will ever eliminate sexual activity when men and women are thrust together at close quarters. Watching civilian and military leaders struggle mightily not to see this verity, I am often reminded of Douglas MacArthur's observation, shortly after arriving in postwar Japan, upon being told that a large number of soldiers had taken up with Japanese women. Asked if such conduct should be curtailed, MacArthur demurred. "I would never give an order that I know I can't enforce," he said.

MacArthur knew that soldiers are usually young, physical, and aggressive, and that from time to time they will find ways to relieve their sexual frustrations with consenting females. But at night MacArthur's soldiers returned to their barracks. And when their units were called upon to perform their missions, the objects of their antics and desires were not right there beside them, confusing their notions of duty, discipline, and sacrifice.

Present-day generals and admirals, constantly under political pressure, sometimes unsure of where to draw the line between military and civilian control, often constrained by legal edicts, and wishing to be fair to those females who do perform well, have issued unenforceable orders rather than confront the politicians who dreamed them up. They have muddled about for years from incident to incident while many junior leaders have been forced to deal directly with impossible, ethically compromising positions. . . .

MILITARY WOMEN OPPOSE COMPLETE INTEGRATION

Who really wants to expand this continued sexual assimilation? A study of soldiers by Harvard researcher Laura Miller suggests that Army women do not. Only 3 percent of the enlisted women surveyed believed they "should be treated exactly like men and serve in the combat arms just like men." Sixty-one percent indicated a belief that sexual harassment would increase if combat billets were opened up to females. An equal percentage believed that women should not be drafted, or should be drafted for service other than close combat. Only 11 percent of enlisted women and 14 percent of the female officers surveyed indicated that they would volunteer for a combat role if one were offered.

These are the realists who have lived in the powder-keg atmosphere. They know precisely what they want out of their military service. They also know precisely those circumstances under which unwanted difficulties arise. Many of them have rightly grown weary of being pawns in the grand schemes of sociologists, agenda feminists, and a small core of political-activist military officers, and of having to live with the often sexually abrasive results of such activism.

The time has finally come to cease examining these issues solely from the perspective of how the military culture should adjust itself to women. While women make valuable contributions on a variety of levels, the military is and always has been a predominantly male profession. Its leaders should demand that any adjustments in sexual roles meet the historically appropriate criterion of improving performance, and should stop salving the egos of a group of never-satisfied social engineers.

STEPS TOWARD NORMALCY

A return to normalcy might cause a retrenchment in areas where women serve. The United States might want to learn from other countries with their own experience of women at arms. After World War II, the Soviet army completely abandoned the use of women in the operating military (they had been brought in owing to the loss of some 7 million male soldiers in combat). The Israelis at several points during their recent history have adjusted the roles of females. Contrary to popular mythology, it is against Israeli law for a woman to serve in combat—and "combat" is a term interpreted far more broadly there than it is here.

A logical first, immediate step for the U.S. military to take is that basic training should be sexually separated, as it has been throughout history until just the past few years. Beyond that, each service chief should order, on his own initiative, a full and honest review of the extent to which current sexual practices are damaging traditional standards of command, discipline, fairness, and cohesion. Where damage is being done, policies should be changed. Where sexual mixing does work, policies should be enhanced. Such a review should not be within the power of civilian service secretaries or members of Congress to obstruct, since "good order and discipline" is the ultimate responsibility of each service chief—a responsibility that many would argue has been abandoned in recent decades when it comes to this issue.

If these senior leaders prove too hamstrung, too compromised, or too politicized to take such action, then the present Congress should take steps similar to those of its Watergate-era predecessor and begin the process of dramatic change itself. Except that this time, the change would be for the purpose of preserving military traditions, values, and leadership rather than subjugating them to external political agendas.

Political and military leaders must have the courage to ask clearly in what areas our current policies toward women in the military are hurting, rather than helping, the task of defending the United States. We have now endured two decades of experimentation, and data on the experiment's results would be voluminous if they were allowed to be examined. It has been a long time since a military leader of virtually any rank was free to speak openly about this without fear of retribution. And the difficulties surrounding the good order and discipline of our armed forces will not abate until the leaders themselves are encouraged not only to point to areas in which the new policy is working, but to speak honestly and straightforwardly about where they are not.

> "When men volunteer for and serve in combat units, they are rightly considered noble. To call women who are trying to do the same 'selfish' is incomprehensible."

WOMEN SHOULD SERVE IN COMBAT

Lillian A. Pfluke

Women in the U.S. armed forces are prohibited from serving in most combat positions. In the following viewpoint, Lillian A. Pfluke argues that this prohibition should be lifted. Pfluke maintains that there is no logical reason for excluding all female soldiers, regardless of ability or qualifications, from combat roles. Military women who are capable of serving in combat should be allowed to do so, she concludes. Pfluke is a mechanical engineer, a freelance writer, and a retired army major.

As you read, consider the following questions:

1. According to the author, what percent of jobs in the U.S. Army and the Marine Corps are closed to women?
2. In Pfluke's opinion, why was the story of Kara Hultgreen's crash widely publicized?
3. What does the all-volunteer force mean, in the author's view?

It's no exaggeration to say that for 22 years women have made the all-volunteer military work. Women are an integral part of the armed forces, about 12 percent of its members. Because of their high aptitude scores, greater propensity to graduate from high school and a level of motivation that defines the high-quality recruits sought by the services, women have replaced many men who want to remain civilians.

MANY JOBS ARE CLOSED TO WOMEN

The military has a screening program to match recruits' abilities with their jobs. Aptitude tests, skills tests, medical screening, physical tests and personal interests all go toward determining a recruit's assignment. All service members meet the same standards in determining what their jobs and assignments will be. There are no separate standards for women or anyone else in determining whether a soldier can do a job.

The only exception is that no matter how qualified, women will not be assigned to certain specialties and to any direct ground-combat units. They are not assigned to any infantry, armor or field-artillery battalions or to any short-range air defense, special forces or combat-engineer companies—not as cooks, not as typists, not as mechanics, not as anything. A full 33 percent of the jobs in the Army and 38 percent of the jobs in the Marine Corps are closed to women. Furthermore, the military does not intend to change that policy and, in fact, cannot change it without first notifying Congress.

Regrettably, a few lobbyists and columnists with little military or national-security experience have begun arguing that women should not remain in those many positions—short of direct ground combat—in which they already are serving effectively. These attacks demean the contributions of thousands of men and women who are proudly serving.

To clarify the issue, let's look at exactly what women are and are not doing in today's armed forces. Recently, Congress and the Defense Department loosened some restrictions not involving direct ground combat. Women now are allowed to serve on more Navy ships, to fly more combat aircraft and to serve in a few more ground-combat-support units.

REPEALING RESTRICTIVE LAWS

But keep in mind that women have flown combat aircraft since aircraft were invented. In World War II, Women Airforce Service Pilots, or WASPs, flew every type of aircraft in the inventory, shuttling them between factories, repair facilities and the theaters of operation. Women started flying Navy jets in 1975. They have been landing on aircraft carriers since 1979. They have been teaching male pilots how to fly combat aircraft since 1980. They have been flying as enemy aircraft in flight schools and training operations as well, engaging in mock dogfights with male pilots. Women have been performing superbly in all types of flight operations, including combat training, for years.

Congress recognized this fact after the Persian Gulf War and repealed the law prohibiting women from flying in combat. This act halted the Navy and the Air Force from the somewhat ludicrous practice of choosing less-qualified male pilots for assignments to fighter and bomber units. The January 1993 announcement allowing women to compete for positions in combat aircraft merely implemented what Congress directed in a convincing bipartisan vote in July 1991.

Don Wright. Reprinted by permission of Tribune Media Services.

Women are allowed to fly most types of aircraft in the Army, Navy, Air Force and Marine Corps. This includes transport jets, propeller planes and helicopters, as well as those aircraft that drop bombs and engage in air-to-air combat. Women are not allowed to fly aircraft in support of some special-forces operations.

Women have been going to sea on Navy ships since 1977 and on Coast Guard ships since 1980. They command vessels, deploy on extended cruises throughout the world and serve successfully in every capacity. (They had been precluded from serving on combat ships on a permanent basis, although they could serve there on a temporary basis and often did.) In 1994, Congress repealed the law prohibiting Navy women from being deployed permanently on combat ships. Women currently serve on most classes of combat ships, except submarines.

The July 1994 announcement by Defense Secretary William Perry opening new jobs for women in the military reaffirmed that women would not serve in direct ground combat. In the Army, however, doors were opened for women to serve in certain military police companies, chemical platoons, smoke platoons, bridge companies, military-intelligence companies, brigade headquarters elements and the Washington-based ceremonial unit—hardly controversial stuff. Gains for women in the Marine Corps were similar. They included more support positions throughout the battlefield—but none in direct ground-combat units in any capacity.

Changing the Rules

Why were some of the old rules changed? In a word, readiness. According to Perry: "Our overachieving goal is to maintain a high-quality, ready and effective force. By increasing the number of units and positions to which women can be assigned, the military services gain greater flexibility in the development and use of human resources. I am confident that these policy changes will further enhance the already-high state of readiness of our armed forces."

The military services are full of smart, competent, well-trained and motivated men and women. The services now can better use their soldiers, sailors, airmen and Marines in the jobs for which each individual is most qualified. On planes and surface ships and in ground-combat-support positions, commanders no longer have to worry about whether a fully qualified individual can or cannot be assigned to a post.

Opponents of women who want to serve their country by fighting for it have been trying to cast these women as radical left-wing feminists. Not true: Military women reflect the military culture they have chosen. They are obedient, dedicated and patriotic. A few may appear restive, but only because they are trying to break through an armored ceiling and be all that they can be. Military women are like their male counterparts, conservative in the true sense.

Did the death of one of the Navy's first female fighter pilots, Lt. Kara Hultgreen, prove that women are poor risks in air combat? Not at all. Hultgreen was killed when her engine stalled as she was attempting to land on a carrier on Oct. 25, 1994. In investigating the accident, the Navy put nine different pilots of various experience levels in a simulator, told them they were about to have a serious incident and simulated an engine stall similar to what killed Hultgreen. Only one man, the unit commander and most experienced pilot to try, survived. Landing an aircraft on a carrier is probably the most difficult maneuver a pilot performs. The Navy and Marine Corps together lose approximately 35 to 40 people a year in aircraft fatalities. The Hultgreen story was publicized widely only because the pilot was a woman and because of an insidious campaign by a small group of lobbyists to denigrate military women, not because a crash on a carrier is unprecedented.

PREGNANCY RATES ARE NOT A PROBLEM

It is true, as reported, that in January 1995 five women were airlifted off the USS Eisenhower because they were pregnant. It is also true, but rarely reported, that 27 men were airlifted off at the same time for various problems. Navy studies conducted during the past decade continue to show that male sailors have lost time from duty at a rate much higher than that of female sailors—even when pregnancy is included.

WOMEN CAN PLAY MANY ROLES

There is a traditionalist view that women enjoy a special status in our society and should be protected, not the protectors. As the givers of life, it is argued, combat is or ought to be against a woman's nature and their principal, though not exclusive, responsibility is to the family. . . .

But, in fact, the idea that women are protected in our society is largely a myth. It is sadly true that women are safer in combat units in the military than they are on the streets of our capital city at night. It is also true that women, as the givers of life, deserve respect. Anyone who can fly an F-18, bear children, and chair the board of a nursery school has mine.

Heather Wilson, National Interest, Summer 1993.

Opponents of combat roles for women conclude that we should restrict women from combat ships (or any military position) because a few become pregnant. This makes as much sense as saying we should prohibit married men because a few may be sent home early for family reasons, or with prostate problems or because they hurt themselves playing basketball. The chief of naval operations, a decorated and respected combat leader with more than 38 years of service, does not view pregnancy and fraternization as a crisis requiring congressional intervention any more than the numerous other personnel issues with which he must deal. Why, then, do certain columnists still claim scandal?

The only real scandal is the constant attempt to politicize the issue and to drag the members of the armed forces into an abstract, ideological fight of antifeminism vs. feminism. The only real shame is that those very few critics of women in the military are reduced to travesties such as denigrating Hultgreen and raising the phony specter of mothers drafted into foxholes.

WOMEN'S REASONS FOR SERVING IN THE MILITARY

Individual rights and personal responsibility define who we are and what we stand for. A female citizen is an individual with the same responsibility and opportunity as male citizens to participate in the national defense, based upon her personal abilities and motivations. Let's remember what the all-volunteer force means: Any person, man or woman, unwilling to take the risks of military service simply chooses not to join.

Women join the military for the same reasons men do: a deep sense of patriotism, a love of country and way of life and a selfless dedication to duty. These are gender-neutral motivations. When men volunteer for and serve in combat units, they are rightly considered noble. To call women who are trying to do the same "selfish" is incomprehensible.

In fact, military service is anything but selfish. Every service member is willing to make the ultimate sacrifice in defense of freedom, country or, as was the case [during the famine relief mission] in Somalia, to be able to help fellow human beings. Women in the service merely want everyone to focus on providing the nation with the best possible defense and to agree on one simple unifying concept: "the best person for the job."

4

"If seeing women come home in the body bags is [feminists'] idea of equality, then we're in deep trouble."

WOMEN SHOULD NOT SERVE IN COMBAT

K.L. Billingsley

Women are not capable of serving in combat roles, K.L. Billingsley maintains in the following viewpoint. Billingsley argues that military experiments with gender-integrated basic training reveal that female recruits rarely meet even the minimum fitness standards expected of the men. Because women lack the physical body strength of men, the author asserts, they will never be able to successfully engage in frontline combat against enemy troops. Opening combat positions to women, Billingsley insists, will simply undermine military readiness and result in unnecessary fatalities. Billingsley is a staff writer for Heterodoxy, a conservative periodical published by the Center for the Study of Popular Culture in Los Angeles, California.

As you read, consider the following questions:

1. According to the author, why can Kara Hultgreen's death be considered Pat Schroeder's first kill?
2. In the opinion of William Gregor, as cited by the author, what percent of women can meet male fitness standards?
3. What examples does Billingsley give of double standards at Forts Jackson and Leonard Wood?

Excerpted from K.L. Billingsley, "Feminist Forced March," Heterodoxy, June 1995; © Heterodoxy 1995. Reprinted by permission of the editors.

The Army recruitment video shows the young men coming to Ft. Leonard Wood in Missouri looking like a bunch of lowlifes about to be arrested for loitering. Then the hair gets sheared as the first step in a change of identity from private citizens to GIs. Recruits find their own will replaced by that of drill sergeants with the temperament of a junkyard Doberman. Then comes boot camp—a grueling marathon of pushups sites, rope climbs, tear gas, marches, and weapons training. The recruits smash each other with pugil sticks and charge through a bayonet course yelling "Kill! Kill!"

By the end of their training, one assumes that Army instructors will have molded this bunch into what recruiting posters used to call "the fighting man." But some versions of the video append a section showing women in basic combat training. The effect is akin to clicking from *The Battle of the Bulge* with Henry Fonda to *Private Benjamin* with Goldie Hawn. When the women run through the bayonet course shrieking "Kill!" and jabbing ineptly at rubber dummies, the effect is unintentionally comic. Some women have trouble with the pins on the grenades, and one doubts that their clumsiness in covering up would have protected them or their fellow soldiers from the blast. Some handle the standard-issue M-16 rifle as though it were a broom.

IGNORING REALITY

The army tape leaves little doubt that any regular troops or guerrilla forces anywhere in the world would quickly slaughter these women. That reality, evident to most veterans of actual combat, has not prevented the return of the "gender-integrated" combat training that is now the keystone of a campaign to move women into front-line combat. Of course, that reality has not deterred left-liberal politicians like Colorado Congressperson Pat Schroeder, for whom current policies are the end of a Long March.

For Schroeder and her feminist comrades in arms—most of whom are, on issues not having to do with women, hardcore anti-military—the issue remains entirely ideological. They believe that if women can't be gassed, shot, blown up, or tortured just like men, they remain incomplete human beings bereft of their constitutional rights. As in other arenas, these feminists confuse equality with sameness in their view of the military and ignore basic realities about the differences between men and women.

Ignoring basic realities, in fact, is probably what accounts for the death of Kara Hultgreen, the first woman to fly a carrier-based F-14 fighter jet. Hultgreen was killed in an abortive landing on October 25, 1994, and at first Schroeder and her allies were able to mislead the press and the public into believing that the problem was mechanical malfunction. But recent evidence, suppressed by the Navy, shows that Hultgreen had recorded seven downs (crashes in combat conditions) during training maneuvers. These failures, which would have long since grounded a male flyer, had been ignored in Hultgreen's case to pacify those like Schroeder who had made women in combat a civil-rights issue. So, the death of Kara Hultgreen was, in some sense, Pat Schroeder's first kill.

It is true, according to Army data, that female recruits are usually better qualified academically than males, have more work experience, and are almost always better behaved, losing less time for disciplinary reasons and not being as inclined as their brethren to abuse drugs and alcohol. But it is also true that soldiering is strenuous business—and women's upper-body strength is roughly half that of a man. They miss more than twice as much duty time on medical grounds and are four times more likely to complain of spurious physical ailments. Women suffer higher rates of attrition and lower rates of retention. The injury rates of women can be as high as 14 times that of men. . . .

AN EXPERIMENT IN GENDER-INTEGRATED TRAINING

In 1978, . . . the Army began an experiment in "gender-integrated training" at Fort Jackson, South Carolina, the largest basic-training facility in the Army. It went on until 1982, when the Army suddenly and somewhat mysteriously dropped it.

Typically, the U.S. Army keeps meticulous records on everything, so a four-year departure from 200 years of standard military practice would likely receive massive scrutiny and documentation. Yet anyone attempting to obtain reports on those four years finds themselves staring into a black hole.

"There is no report about 1978 to 1982," Jacqueline Mottern, a social psychologist with the Army Research Institute told me. "We can find no written document as to why the Army canceled that project in 1982. There is nothing in the archives to explain what happened or why it happened." Mottern, who said she was unable to refer me to a single person involved in that project, concedes that the absence of records is "unusual."

It also happens to be false. "It's impossible that there are no records; they have been lost on purpose," says Korean war veteran Col. Robert Maginnis, now retired and working with the Family Research Council in Washington, D.C. Working outside official channels, I was finally able to locate a senior military official who was one of the first to supervise the training of women as well as a captain and a colonel who had taken part in the first gender-integration project—all three of them so concerned about how taking the wrong position on gender correctness can wreck a career or even a retirement that they requested anonymity.

A COMPLETE DISASTER

"It was a disaster, plain and simple," says the captain, "absolute abject failure . . . beyond stupid." While the Army concedes that there may have been "a perception that the men were not being physically challenged enough," the captain responds, "it was not a perception, even the troops said it. They would run a while, stop, then sit and wait for the women. It was 'keep up with the slowest.'" He describes women breaking down in tears during the basic training, especially on the rifle range, as commonplace. Or, in his own words, "They would come unglued."

Reprinted by permission of Chuck Asay and Creators Syndicate.

On the grenade course, the soldier stands five feet away from a seven-foot-high wall, over which he or she must toss a grenade. "I've watched the women bounce hand grenades off the wall," the captain says.

"They broke into tears in a flash," says the senior military official, one of the first to supervise the training of female soldiers. He adds that their very presence, segregated or integrated, affected the men. "The men want to believe that very few can do what they are doing, that they are being challenged to a point where only a few succeed. They are told that the women have to be allowed to do it too. That's just shattering to them."

Tests Reveal Serious Shortcomings

After the Army stopped the gender integration without explanation in 1982, it went back to separate training for men and women. But the debate continued, along with the search for accurate data. A study by Dr. David Robertson at Navy Personnel Research and Development Center in San Diego tested 350 male and 195 female recruits in such damage-control tasks as carrying litters on level surfaces and up and down ladders, moving and starting emergency pumps, turning engine bolts, and directing fire-hose streams. Virtually all of the male recruits were able to perform all of the tasks to standard, even before training, but the only task most female recruits could perform to standard was directing a fire hose, and even after significant training 99 percent of the women could still not carry a pump down a ladder.

"The Navy's recent enthusiasm for putting more and more women aboard ship makes little sense," says Paul O. Davis, "unless the Navy doesn't mind sacrificing survivability and possibly the lives of its sailors for the sake of enhancing opportunities for women." Davis was the principal investigator of the multi-year study to validate the Marine Corps Physical Fitness test and also served as the lead instructor of the Navy's training and certification program for Command Fitness Coordinators.

The invasion of Panama in December 1989 gave new impetus for lifting combat restrictions for women, but the Gulf War proved the real watershed in this movement within the military. The Pentagon and media praised the performance of the 35,000 women who served in that conflict. But as sociologist Charles Moskos points out, surveys of soldiers yield a murkier picture: "Over half rated women's performance as fair or poor."

Women's Best Is Not Good Enough

This was not merely a subjective assessment. In September 1992, Col. William Gregor, professor of advanced military studies at Fort Leavenworth, testified to the Presidential Commission on the Assignment of Women in the Military that the Army Physical Fitness Test (APFT) showed that the women who pass standards are already at the upper end of the female population's potential. "Additional training, even Herculean efforts," said Gregor, "will not significantly change the results." These results showed that, with a few weeks' additional training, the most marginal male recruit can surpass the performance of the best-trained women. Gregor also noted that adopting a male standard of fitness would mean that 70 percent of women would fail and no one would receive an Army Physical Fitness Badge because not a single woman achieved a score equal to what men must meet to get the badge.

In 1993, the Marine Corps conducted a three-month study with 50 women to determine whether they could be conditioned to meet male fitness standards. Details of the study are sketchy, but an *Army Times* article notes that "officials found that they could not be." While some women can reach the lower ranges of male ability, they are operating at the peak of their performance and are therefore under maximum stress. Col. Gregor testified that finding one woman out of 100 who can meet standards as opposed to 60 percent of men who can means that that Army has in effect "just traded off 60 soldiers for the prospect of getting one.". . .

SETTING DOUBLE STANDARDS

Secretary of the Army Togo West, an engineer and lawyer with only four years of military experience (and that in a bureaucratic role), has revived the gender-integrated training which was such a disaster in the 1978–82 period. . . . An Army press release says that "all training will be without favoritism and accomplished to Army standards." But in light of what is going on at Forts Jackson and Leonard Wood, that can only be a reference to "dual standards."

For example, men are required to do 32 pushups in two minutes, the women 13. The obstacle course for women is different, and the required time for the two-mile run is slower. And the present experiment is finding some of the same realities about female psychology and physiology as the previous attempt in 1978–82.

"You find the women are more emotional," Lt. Col. Ron Perry of Fort Leonard Wood told the *Washington Post*. "For instance, when they stand on the rifle range and are told they've failed, many of the women will break down, while the guys will kick a stone and curse."

Military brass staunchly deny it, but there is abundant evidence that gender-integrated training has lowered standards across the board. As the *Detroit News* pointed out, at Fort Knox recruits have traded combat boots for running shoes and are now allowed to go around a 6-foot wall they were previously required to scale. Formerly mandatory overnight bivouacs may now be canceled because of bad weather. And one training march avoids Heartbreak Hill, which some deemed too tough.

At Fort Leonard Wood, Pvt. Vanessa Overhaus, a 19-year-old from Buffalo, broke down and cried on the first day of training. Then she fell five times on the bayonet course, forcing several officers to walk her through the maneuver. A full seven tries later, she scaled the wall. Like most of the women, she now feels better about herself, but her physical limitations remain.

There are social factors as well as physical ones. Even the most generous press reports acknowledge continual complaints from the women over bathroom and shower facilities. Sgt. Steven Buie of Fort Leonard Wood said that higher rates of injuries and sick call with female trainees have handicapped training, as they did in the 1978–82 experiment. The male recruits know that the drill sergeants would be much tougher on them without women around.

No Need for Women in Combat

Army spokesperson Jacqueline Mottern echoes Army claims that all is well, that everybody in the military loves the policy, and that the women are performing as well as the men. But according to Col. Robert Maginnis and other critics of the feminization of the military, performance can only be rated equal by changing definitions of cohesion and "soldierization." Maginnis says, "They changed the whole modus operandi as to how you measure performance. Before it was physical, now they measure nonphysical, map reading, first aid. When you gender-norm these things, the women will come out at or above the level of men."

Women make up about 12 percent of America's 1.5 million troops on active duty, a greater proportion than of any other nation. According to Col. William Gregor, however, there is no real need for current policies. "We arbitrarily exclude 40 percent of our men from military service," he says. "Having blocked suitable males from enlistment, does it then make sense to adopt special training methods to make women more like men? Given declining training budgets, why should the Army embark on a specialized training effort to achieve what normal training methods would otherwise do?"

The former Army trainers hold no doubt that the PC [politically correct] contingent in Congress and its allies in the Defense Advisory Committee on Women in the Service will be satisfied with nothing less than women in front-line combat. Yet unlike the PC forces these men have actually engaged in combat and understand what the new policy will mean. They estimate that the current gender-integrated training has reduced our readiness by 5 percent and that women in combat would reduce it by 30 percent.

PERVERTING MILITARY INTEGRITY AND READINESS

"This is social engineering at its worst," says former Navy secretary James Webb, a Vietnam vet whose article, "Women Can't Fight," got him banned from the Naval Academy for four years. (Possession of the article, members of a presidential commission were told, can constitute sexual harassment at the academies.) "The problem in purely objective terms is that it doesn't stress the men. Females fall behind in the aggregate and you basically water down the training." Webb adds that "the greatest damage of this issue is the way the political process has perverted the sense of integrity of the officer corps. When the commander of a ship stands up in front of the world and says none of these pregnancies occurred on board ship, every sailor in the Navy knows they are lying. When you see your leaders as hypocrites, integrity goes out the window."

In his early days as a comic, Bill Cosby had a funny routine about a referee who handed out the rules of engagement before every war. But real warfare is no laughing matter, and there are no referees. In a real war, Vanessa Overhaus will have only one chance, not seven, to get over the obstacle, and when she fails she will be shot dead along with those males lending her a hand. Their blood will cry out from the ground, all the way to the Capitol Hill offices of Pat Schroeder and her comrades who have been engaging in their own war against nature on this issue.

"Unfortunately, we are going to have to get a lot of people killed before what these people have done is clear," says the captain who participated in the ill-fated 1978 gender-integration experiment. "If seeing women come home in the body bags is their idea of equality, then we're in deep trouble—in this society and in the military which protects it."

> "I have listened in quiet frustration to men who say women don't belong in the cockpit—when we are already there."

FEMALE AVIATORS ARE CAPABLE OF FLYING COMBAT MISSIONS

Lin Hutton

Military women were barred from flying fighter jets in combat units until April 28, 1993, when Les Aspin, then the secretary of defense, issued a memorandum that lifted the ban. In the following viewpoint, Lin Hutton praises Aspin's decision and defends the ability of women to fly warplanes. She points out that for many years female pilots have flown fighter planes in training and testing situations and that they regularly are assigned to other types of military aircraft. These women are entitled to the right to compete with men for combat aviation positions, Hutton maintains, and to win such assignments based on their individual merits and skill. At the time this viewpoint was written, Hutton was the commanding officer of Fleet Logistics Support Squadron Forty, a naval carrier aviation squadron based in Norfolk, Virginia.

As you read, consider the following questions:

1. In Hutton's opinion, what do dedicated sailors seek?
2. How many naval specialties and fields were open to women in 1993, according to the author?
3. What response does Hutton offer to the argument that Americans will not tolerate women being killed in combat?

"The times they are a-changin'." I heard that refrain countless times as I grew up in the '60s and '70s. Today, I recall it with great pride—and hope—for so many hardworking and talented American women in the military. In a sweeping policy memorandum issued on April 28, 1993, Secretary of Defense Les Aspin has directed the armed services to allow women to compete for assignments in aircraft engaged in combat missions. For so many of us, this is a long-awaited change. Since 1973, women have served successfully and proudly in the demanding field of naval aviation. Now, after 20 years, we have the chance to be fully integrated into our profession—to fly planes like the F-14 Tomcat in any situation, not just for training and testing.

Paving the Way

In 1976, I was designated the seventh woman naval aviator in U.S. history. I am proud to know I was among the "first." I'm also proud to be a naval officer currently in command of a carrier aviation squadron of 13 aircraft and nearly 350 outstanding young Americans, one third of whom are women. We fly C-2A "Greyhound" transport planes, carrying personnel and supplies from ship to shore. I myself have made more than 360 carrier landings and have logged nearly 4,000 flight hours. I believe I have played a small part in paving a road for others to follow. Though it's too late for me to aim for the F-14, many young women can now look forward to it. How I wish I were in their shoes!

Throughout my 18 years of naval service I have worked with men and women from all over our country. I've learned the dedicated sailor seeks only to do a job without fear of discrimination or harassment. I can remember when such circumstances were impossible. I was born in 1951, the daughter of a navy pilot who moved his family every two years. As a child I saw that African-Americans and Filipino service members were not pilots or technicians. They were cooks and compartment cleaners, stewards and messmen. What a tragic waste of human talent.

I watched the civil-rights movement change our world. I learned in school about a landmark decision by the Supreme Court in 1954 called Brown v. Board of Education of Topeka. I learned the great phrase "separate but equal is not equal" and for the last 18 years have wondered why this is true for different races but not for men and women.

Tremendous Change

And it seems, at last, that this, too, is changing. Even before [Aspin's] historic decision, I have seen tremendous change, particularly in the navy. When I first received my gold aviator wings, women were not permitted to land on any ship in any type of aircraft. Today, women fly planes like I do all around the world, replenishing our ships at sea and contributing in countless other ways day and night to the national defense. Eighty out of 96 specialties are open to enlisted women, and all but two fields (special forces and submarines) are open to women officers. Navy women have assimilated themselves well in those ships and squadrons currently open to their assignment. In my squadron alone, I have five women aviators and six women aircrew. Four of them, along with 29 other men and women, recently returned from a six-month deployment to the Mediterranean with the USS *John F. Kennedy* Battlegroup.

No Physical Limitations

In the decades since women became part of military aviation, concerns over their impact have been fading. Researchers had found no physical reason why a man would be superior to a woman as a jet pilot. In fact, because women tend to be shorter, the heart generally has a smaller distance to pump blood to the brain and it is easier to withstand the short bursts of extra gravity that can drive consciousness away during acceleration and turns.

Judy Pasternak, *Los Angeles Times*, May 11, 1993.

In all sorts of weather, they flew more than 1,000 hours in 700 sorties, carrying more than 5,000 passengers and 1.4 million pounds of cargo, much of it in the Adriatic in support of Operation Deny Flight (the no-fly zone over Bosnia). The success of the mission resulted not from the work of any one individual but from the work of the entire team.

On the way back to the United States, the squadron detachment, composed of 12 women and 21 men, returned home aboard the aircraft carrier *John F. Kennedy*. There were no incidents of harassment, discrimination or improper conduct.

Women Can Do the Job

The majority of our nation's sailors are dedicated professionals who routinely work more than 100 hours a week at sea. There is little time or patience for those who will not or cannot pull their own load. If the women could not do the job, they would not be there. And I believe that basic premise forms the root of "unit cohesion."

Since 1978, women have served on naval ships. They have sought the same goals as their male counterparts: to earn money for college, to learn a technical skill, to travel and see the world; and yes, to serve their country in the noblest profession, where they place their lives between their country and harm. Perhaps the ultimate irony is that women and men are more alike than they are different.

I have listened in quiet frustration to men who say women don't belong in the cockpit—when we are already there. I have listened to men say, "Americans won't tolerate women coming home in body bags"—when women already have. And I believe the tragedy of body bags is devastating to any family, regardless of the race or gender of the departed soul. Perhaps if the world were as horrified of men being killed in combat as they presumably are of women, we might not fight as many wars. But until that happens, let's ensure that many of our brightest and best are not overlooked in their aspirations to contribute.

| *"Anybody who says technology levels the playing field, and gender matters not, has never been in sustained, life-threatening combat."*

FEMALE AVIATORS ARE NOT CAPABLE OF FLYING COMBAT MISSIONS

Jerry R. Cadick

In the following viewpoint, Jerry R. Cadick argues that women are not physically or emotionally capable of handling combat roles, and especially not the extremely dangerous job of fighter pilot. A retired marine colonel, Vietnam veteran, and fighter pilot, Cadick maintains that although some women are good aviators, they cannot meet the high standards expected of a fighter pilot. Furthermore, he insists, male combat aviators will never trust their female peers in wartime situations. Cadick concludes that the military opened warplane assignments to women due to pressure from civilians and politicians who have faulty conceptions about the nature of air warfare and women's ability to perform it.

As you read, consider the following questions:

1. How does Cadick depict the environment of a fighter pilot?
2. How does the author describe the history of female warriors?
3. What will happen if women are let into air squadrons, in the author's view?

From Jerry R. Cadick, "On Being a Warrior," *Newsweek*, April 14, 1997; ©1997, Newsweek, Inc. All rights reserved. Reprinted by permission.

I am an American citizen. But I'm also a United States Marine Corps Fighter Pilot. Retired, yes, but the nature of the business is so intense that those of us who are cannot ever claim that we "used to be." It's impossible to explain what it is to be one of us without experiencing it. Since retiring, I have been an airshow pilot, an entrepreneur and a substitute teacher. However, I am still—and will be until I die—a Fighter Pilot, a Warrior.

I'm sure you've seen the Hollywood version. Probably you've been to an air show and been dazzled by the death-defying maneuvers and simulated military strikes. A few of us have actually gone through the gauntlet in which the few became even fewer and were christened Fighter Pilots.

A LIFE GAMBLE

Where we work is a vicious place. I'll attempt to describe it, but real comprehension comes only in a sky full of hot metal and smart missiles that all seem to be looking right at you. You're in a machine that is so fast and powerful that you instinctively know that if death comes, it will be full of hot fire. Frail human that you are, you will be shred into bits and pieces. Worst of all, you'll be alone in a fierce place where your comrades cannot hold on to you while you die.

That is the real environment of a Fighter Pilot. It's a life gamble in which only a few can thrive. The citizenry and the government sense enough of the hazard so that praise aplenty awaits those foolish enough to do it. We accept the attention because we are the elite defenders of our nation. But Fighter Pilots, of necessity, camp outside the back door of Hades, and that can get us into trouble—witness the Tailhook Convention. [The 1991 Tailhook Convention received media attention and an official investigation due to reports of widespread sexual harassment and assault.] We live on the edge and, guess what, we play there, too.

A few words on Tailhook. I was once a board member of that august body. (Liberals, heat up your word processors.) I was elected after running against the Navy's only Vietnam Ace, Cmdr. Randy Cunningham, now a congressman and a fine man in my opinion. The 1991 convention was the Navy's wake-up call to "political correctness." For years, we got together and behaved like the barbarians that our profession demanded of us. It was not harmless, but it sure as hell was consistent with the Gamble to which we had sworn allegiance. We buried one out of four who tried to make a 20-year career (I came within a red-hair-breadth of being buried), and, by God, we had no inclination to be conservative about this trip on the "Blue Marble" (planet Earth).

WOMEN ARE NOT WARRIORS

Citizens, or their elected representatives, believe that women can be Fighter Pilots. Reasons abound why this should be. Equality is foremost. Politicians weave tales wherein the physical differences, being moot in the cockpit, make that place ideal for a woman. They say that if she can complete the training, then, by cracky, she is qualified. In 26 years in the USMC, some of the most skilled officers in the five units that I commanded were women. I knew some female Naval Aviators, and they were pilots as good as can be found in the nose of any American passenger airliner. If we talk about flying (the art of) from point A to point B, then many humans qualify handily.

But we ain't talking about flying here. We gotta get down to basics, like where we evolved from and some *real hard* natural-selection rules Mother Nature wrote in her Standard Operating Procedures manual.

WOMEN THREATEN FIGHTER SQUADRON EFFICIENCY

When you are out there in your fleet squadron, it is very important that you act as one, and you believe and you share your experiences with each and every member, and you expect a lot out of that person, and you have to act as a unit. And if you can't do that—and we don't believe that you can act as a unit unless you keep it the way it is, where it's the bonding—it's that intangible, the bonding, that makes a squadron good, better, and we don't believe you can have that go on if we have females in aviation.

John Clagett, quoted by Jean Zimmerman in *Tailspin:Women at War in the Wake of Tailhook*, 1995.

Has there ever been a major culture where women were the elite warriors? How about just warriors? Apache women sometimes fought alongside the men. I know of a female Russian battalion that fought against Germany (they damn near all died). Israel has a bit of experience (they say never again). But I am unaware of any historical precedent, except on a limited scale. That oughta tell us something, and I haven't begun to talk about reasons, based on experience, that females in combat ain't good.

Anybody who says technology levels the playing field, and gender matters not, has never been in sustained, life-threatening combat. Technology matters not a whit. The human response that gripped our ancestors' stomachs and made them want to vomit when they crossed stone axes was, I betcha, identical to mine diving into the hell called North Vietnam.

MALE FIGHTER PILOTS WILL NOT ACCEPT WOMEN

I have a fire in my belly that I need to ventilate in the direction of the highly qualified generals and admirals who wear the stars. I say to them: you cannot sit down at a bar as we used to do after flying, look me in the face and say that a female in the carrier Fighter Pilot cockpit, or roundtable, is fine by you—and you know it. You let women (and I happen to love them as a male, but I'll wager I'm in for a dry spell) in the squadrons and on the ships, and you are doing your best to contain the near rebellion among the men. I remember your favorite saying back when you were in the cockpit: "The threat is inversely proportional to the bulls--t." If you utter it today, you'll need a mirror to gaze into. I'm not gonna tell you the right thing to do on account that you already know.

Fighter Pilots, above all else, know who among their peers are "hunters" and who are the "hunted." They absolutely will not fly into a known tough combat situation with a wingman they don't trust, and not all men make the cut. Something akin to bonding has to occur in this ancient ritual called war. The few female Naval Aviators are complaining about being on the outside looking in. The media are starting to tar and feather the Navy for lack of zeal in the stampede toward correctness. Guess what, you are bumping up against millions of years of genetic conditioning. Good F——ing Luck!

Do not fall into the trap of thinking that if someone can hack it in training, it will translate into an effective combatant. The only test of who can function in combat is combat. In war, first order of business, throw damn near all peacetime training rules overboard. All combat veterans know of plenty of situations where someone was eased into a noncombat function on account of not having what it takes. What it takes wasn't written anywhere, but we knew.

Periodical Bibliography

The following articles have been selected to supplement the diverse views presented in this chapter. Addresses are provided for periodicals not indexed in the *Readers' Guide to Periodical Literature*, the *Alternative Press Index*, the *Social Sciences Index*, or the *Index to Legal Periodicals and Books*.

Robert A. Condry — "Are the Services Keeping Women in Their Place?" *Conservative Review*, March/April 1997. Available from 1307 Dolley Madison Blvd., Room 203, McLean, VA 22101.

John Corry — "Dames at Sea," *American Spectator*, August 1996.

Craig Donegan — "New Military Culture," *CQ Researcher*, April 26, 1996. Available from Congressional Quarterly, 1414 22nd St. NW, Washington, DC 20037.

Elaine Donnelly — "Social Experimentation in the Military," *Heritage Lectures*, #522 (speech delivered March 3, 1995). Available from the Heritage Foundation, 214 Massachusetts Ave. NE, Washington, DC 20002-4999.

Cynthia Enloe — "The Right to Fight: A Feminist Catch-22," *Ms.*, July/August 1993.

Suzanne Fields — "Our Coed Army," *Washington Times*, November 18, 1996. Available from 3600 New York Ave. NE, Washington, DC 20002.

Stephanie Gutmann — "Sex and the Soldier," *New Republic*, February 24, 1997.

Issues and Controversies on File — "Women in the Military," June 13, 1997. Available from Facts on File News Services, 11 Penn Plaza, New York, NY 10001-2006.

Peter T. Kilborn — "Sex Abuse Cases Stun Pentagon, but the Problem Has Deep Roots," *New York Times*, February 10, 1997.

R. Cort Kirkwood — "Life on the Front Lines," *Chronicles*, March 1994. Available from the Rockford Institute, 934 N. Main St., Rockford, IL 61103.

Adam G. Merserau — "'Diversity' May Prove Deadly on the Battlefield," *Wall Street Journal*, November 14, 1996.

Ronald D. Ray   "An Absolute Standard," *The New American*, June 12, 1995. Available from 395 Concord Ave., Belmont, MA 02178.

Richard Rayner   "The Warrior Besiegeda," *New York Times Magazine*, June 22, 1997.

Elizabeth Ross   "How Great a Role Should Women Play in Combat?" *Christian Science Monitor*, January 28, 1994.

Rowan Scarborough   "Women Grow Combative in Gender War," *Insight*, April 17, 1995. Available from 3600 New York Ave. NE, Washington, DC 20002.

Eric Schmitt   "Navy Women Bringing New Era on Carriers," *New York Times*, February 21, 1994.

Barbara Vobejda and Thomas Heath   "Opening New Horizons for Women," *Washington Post National Weekly Edition*, May 3–9, 1993. Available from Reprints, 1150 15th St. NW, Washington, DC 20071.

Douglas Waller   "Life on the Coed Carrier," *Time*, April 17, 1995.

For Further Discussion

Chapter 1

1. Linda Chavez argues that women's increased participation in the workforce has harmed society, while Caryl Rivers and Rosalind C. Barnett contend that working women benefit their families and communities. Which viewpoint do you most strongly agree with, and why?

2. Marc Breslow incorporates an interview with two former factory workers as part of his argument that maquiladoras exploit working women. The editors of *Society* use the results of a study to support their contention that maquiladoras benefit women workers. Which author's technique do you find more compelling? Explain.

3. Brenda Hunter contends that children's emotional development can be impaired by their working mothers' absence from home. Diane Eyer claims that the theory that children need to bond with stay-at-home mothers is unfounded. Does Eyer's viewpoint effectively refute Hunter's argument? Why or why not?

Chapter 2

1. Barbara F. Reskin and Irene Padavic maintain that women face pervasive discrimination in the workplace. Michael Lynch and Katherine Post disagree, contending that women do not face significant pay inequities or barriers to advancement. What evidence do these authors present to support their arguments? Which viewpoint contains the most convincing evidence? Support your answers with examples from the viewpoints.

2. The Federal Glass Ceiling Commission argues that women face obstacles—collectively referred to as the "glass ceiling"— in advancing to upper-level management positions. Diana Furchtgott-Roth contends that the glass ceiling is a myth promoted by those who support unfair preferential treatment for female workers. Both authors incorporate statistical data to back up their conclusions. In your opinion, which author's use of statistics is more effective? Explain your answer.

3. Danielle Crittenden maintains that the demanding nature of motherhood, not discrimination, is responsible for working mothers' limited opportunities and lower wages. Are you persuaded by Crittenden's argument that working mothers should not expect to receive the same pay and promotions that men do? Why or why not?

4. Ann Menasche argues that women need affirmative action to overcome present-day discrimination in the workplace; Elizabeth Larson contends that affirmative action for women is unnecessary and counterproductive. Compare their opinions, then formulate your own assessment of the feasibility of gender-based affirmative action.

Chapter 3

1. L.A. Winokur, arguing that sexual harassment is a serious problem for women, characterizes such behavior as "an abuse of power." Elizabeth Larson maintains that what many call sexual harassment is merely "boorish or inappropriate" behavior. Whose argument do you find more persuasive, and why?

2. Maggie Gallagher contends that the integration of women into the military has created an atmosphere in which sexual harassment is inevitable. Harry Summers Jr. argues that if proper military conduct were maintained, women could be integrated without the threat of sexual harassment. Do you think each author's gender is a factor in shaping his or her point of view? Are their arguments unexpected? Whose viewpoint is more compelling? Explain your answers to all these questions.

Chapter 4

1. James Webb objects to women's integration into the military in general, while Dana Priest gives a positive account of the daily working environment of a specific integrated military troop in the field. Do you think Priest effectively answers Webb's points? Why or why not? In your opinion, are Webb's objections applicable to the type of situation that Priest describes? Explain.

2. List some of the examples that K.L. Billingsley provides to argue that women are not capable of fighting in combat situations. What examples does Lillian A. Pfluke give to assert that women can serve in combat? Whose use of examples do you find more convincing? Why? Based on these examples, do you think Billingsley and Pfluke are talking about the same types of combat? Explain your answer.

3. Compare the viewpoints of Lin Hutton and Jerry R. Cadick. For each viewpoint, list the arguments that are based on logical reasoning and those that contain appeals to emotion. In your opinion, which author's argument is more grounded in logic and which uses more emotional appeals? Defend your answer, using examples from the viewpoints.

ORGANIZATIONS TO CONTACT

The editors have compiled the following list of organizations concerned with the issues debated in this book. The descriptions are derived from materials provided by the organizations. All have publications or information available for interested readers. The list was compiled on the date of publication of the present volume; names, addresses, phone and fax numbers, and e-mail and Internet addresses may change. Be aware that many organizations take several weeks or longer to respond to inquiries, so allow as much time as possible.

Center for Research on Women
Wellesley College
106 Central St., Wellesley, MA 02181-8259
(617) 283-2500 • fax: (617) 283-2504
e-mail: lpalmer@wellesley.edu
Internet: http://www.wellesley.edu/WCW/wcwhome.html

The center is dedicated to preventing psychological problems and enhancing of the psychological well-being of women by means of research studies, projects, and publications. Researchers at the center conduct interdisciplinary studies that examine the lives of women, men, and children around the world. Information gathered by the center is provided to individuals and institutions in an effort to bring about policies and practices that benefit women. The center publishes the *Research Report* twice a year.

Clearinghouse on Women's Issues
PO Box 70603, Friendship Heights, MD 20813
(301) 871-6160

The clearinghouse disseminates information on matters concerning women, with particular emphasis on public policies affecting the economic and educational status of women. It publishes the monthly newsletter *Clearinghouse on Women's Issues*.

Coalition on Human Needs (CHN)
1000 Wisconsin Ave. NW, Washington, DC 20007
(202) 342-0726 • fax: (202) 338-1856
e-mail: chn@chn.org

The coalition is an alliance of over 170 national organizations that promote public policies addressing the needs of low-income and other vulnerable populations, such as children, women, the elderly, and people with disabilities. The coalition's members include civil rights, religious, labor, and professional organizations as well as grassroots groups across the country. CHN publishes the biweekly legislative update *Human Needs Report* (when Congress is in session); timely publications, such as the *Welfare Implementation Update*; resource materials, such as the *Directory of National Human Needs Organizations*; and a variety of other informational materials.

Concerned Women for America (CWA)

370 L'Enfant Promenade SW, Suite 800, Washington, DC 20024
(800) 323-2200
Internet: http://www.cwfa.org

CWA's purpose is to preserve, protect, and promote traditional Judeo-Christian values through education, legislative action, and other activities. Its members believe that feminism has harmed society by encouraging women's participation in the workforce, promoting divorce as a symbol of freedom, and endorsing the use of child day care. CWA publishes the monthly *Family Voice* in addition to brochures, booklets, and manuals on numerous issues, including feminism and working women.

Eagle Forum

PO Box 618, Alton, IL 62002
(618) 462-5415
Internet: http://www.otago.ac.nz/qrd/www/RRR/eagle.html

The Eagle Forum is dedicated to preserving traditional family values. It promotes the belief that mothers should stay at home with their children, and it endorses policies that support the traditional family and reduce government intervention in family issues. The forum opposes feminism, arguing that the movement has harmed women and families. The organization publishes the monthly *Phyllis Schlafly Report*.

Families and Work Institute

330 Seventh Ave., New York, NY 10001
(212) 465-2044 • fax: (212) 465-8637
Internet: http://www.familiesandwork.org

The institute is a research and planning organization that develops new approaches to balancing the continuing need for workplace productivity with the changing needs of American families. More than forty research reports are available for sale from the institute, including *The Changing Workforce: Highlights of the National Study, Women: The New Providers, Community Mobilization: Strategies to Support Young Children and Their Families*, and *An Examination of the Impact of Family-Friendly Policies on the Glass Ceiling*.

Family Research Council

700 13th St. NW, Suite 500, Washington, DC 20005
(202) 393-2100 • fax: (202) 393-2134
e-mail: corrdept@frc.org • Internet: http://www.frc.org

The council is a conservative public policy organization that provides information to the public on issues such as parental responsibility, the impact of working parents on children, and the effects of the tax system on families. Its publications include the monthly *Washington Watch*, the bimonthly *Family Policy*, reports, and policy analyses.

Heritage Foundation

214 Massachusetts Ave. NE, Washington, DC 20002
(202) 546-4400 • fax: (202) 544-2260

The Heritage Foundation is a public policy research institute that advocates limited government and the free market system. It opposes affirmative action for women and minorities and believes the private sector, not government, should be relied upon to ease social problems and improve the status of women. The foundation publishes the quarterly journal *Policy Review* as well as hundreds of monographs, books, and papers on public policy issues.

Mothers at Home (MAH)

8310A Old Courthouse Rd., Vienna, VA 22182
(800) 783-4666 • fax: (703) 790-8587
e-mail: MAH@netrail.net • Internet: http://www.mah.org

Mothers at Home is a national organization that strives to enable women to stay home and take care of their children rather than enter the workforce. Its members oppose the view that every woman should have a job and a career. MAH helps women become at-home mothers by offering them support, education, and networking, and it provides the public with education and public policy analysis. It publishes the monthly journal *Welcome Home* and several books, including *What's a Smart Woman Like You Doing at Home?*, *Motherhood: Journey into Love*, and *Discovering Motherhood*.

National Committee on Pay Equity (NCPE)

1126 16th St. NW, Suite 411, Washington, DC 20036
(202) 331-7343 • fax: (202) 331-7406
Internet: http://www.feminist.com/fairpay.html

NCPE is a national coalition of labor, women's, and civil rights organizations and individuals working to achieve pay equity by eliminating sex- and race-based wage discrimination. Its publications include a quarterly newsletter, *Newsnotes*, and numerous books and briefing papers on the issue of pay equity.

National Organization for Women (NOW)

1000 16th St. NW, Suite 700, Washington, DC 20036
(202) 331-0066 • fax: (202) 785-8576
e-mail: now@now.org • Internet: http://www.now.org

NOW is one of the largest women's organizations in the nation. Through education and litigation, it supports equal rights for women, equal pay for women workers, and affirmative action. NOW advocates equality for military servicewomen and favors allowing women to serve in combat roles. The organization publishes the bimonthly *NOW Times*.

9to5 National Association of Working Women

614 Superior Ave. NW, Rm. 852, Cleveland, OH 44113-1387
(216) 566-9308 • fax: (216) 566-0192

The association is the leading membership organization for working women. It utilizes class-action lawsuits and public information campaigns to achieve change on issues including discrimination against pregnant women, sexual harassment in the workplace, and pay equity. It publishes books and reports on topics such as contingent work and sexual harassment; several pamphlets, including the *New 9to5 Office*

Worker Survival Guide; and the newsletters *9to5 Newsline* (twice a month) and *9to5 Profile of Working Women* (once a year).

Rockford Institute
934 Main St., Rockford, IL 61103-7061
(815) 964-5053 • fax: (815) 965-1826
e-mail: rkfdinst@bossnt.com

The institute seeks to return America to Judeo-Christian and traditional family values by educating the public on religious and social issues. It promotes the view that day care is harmful to children and that every effort should be made to allow mothers to raise their children at home. The organization advocates home-based business as one way of allowing mothers to stay at home. Rockford publishes the monthly monograph *The Family in America* and its supplement *New Research*, the monthly magazine *Chronicles,* and the newsletter *Mainstreet Memorandum.*

United Nations Development Fund for Women (UNIFEM)
304 E. 45th St., 6th Fl., New York, NY 10017
(212) 906-6400
e-mail: chutchin@ingenia.com • Internet: http://unifem.ingenia.com

The United Nations Development Fund for Women provides direct support for women's projects and promotes the inclusion of women in the decision-making process of development programs throughout the world. UNIFEM provides these services through its various chapters, namely, UNIFEM in Africa, UNIFEM in Asia and the Pacific, UNIFEM in Latin America and the Caribbean, and UNIFEM at the Global Level. It publishes the monthly newsletters *UNIFEM News* and the *Canadian Committee News.*

Women's International League for Peace and Freedom (WILPF)
1213 Race St., Philadelphia, PA 19107-1697
(215) 563-7110 • fax: (215) 563-5527
e-mail: wilpfnatl@igc.apc.org

WILPF is an international network of women activists who oppose militarism. While it supports equal rights for women, it believes that neither men nor women should participate in the military. WILPF publishes the bimonthly magazine *Peace and Freedom* and the book *The Women's Budget.*

Women Work! The National Network for Women's Employment
1625 K St. NW, Suite 300, Washington, DC 20006
(202) 467-6346 • (800) 235-2732 • fax: (202) 467-5366
e-mail: womenwork@worldnet.att.net

Women Work! fosters the development of programs and services that prepare women for the workforce. It acts as a clearinghouse, providing the public with technical assistance, information, data collection, legislative monitoring, and other services. It also provides referrals and information on research in progress. Women Work! publishes books, guides, reports, the quarterly newsletters *The More Things Change . . . A Status Report on Displaced Homemakers and Single Parents* and *Network News,* and the semiannual newsletter *Women Work!*

BIBLIOGRAPHY OF BOOKS

Titus E. Aaron with
Judith A. Isaksen

Sexual Harassment in the Workplace: A Guide to the Law and a Research Overview for Employers and Employees. Jefferson, NC: McFarland, 1993.

Mimi Abramovitz

Under Attack, Fighting Back: Women and Welfare in the U.S. New York: Monthly Review Press, 1996.

Carol Lee Bacchi

The Politics of Affirmative Action: "Women," Equality, and Category Politics. Thousand Oaks, CA: Sage, 1996.

Rosalind C. Barnett
and Caryl Rivers

She Works, He Works: How Two-Income Families Are Happier, Healthier, and Better-Off. San Francisco: HarperSanFrancisco, 1996.

Sandra Lipsitz Bem

The Lenses of Gender: Transforming the Debate on Sexual Inequality. New Haven, CT: Yale University Press, 1993.

Mary Frances Berry

The Politics of Parenthood: Child Care, Women's Rights, and the Myth of the Good Mother. New York: Viking, 1993.

Barbara Boxer
and Nicole Boxer

Strangers in the Senate: Politics and the New Revolution of Women in America. Washington, DC: National Press Books, 1994.

Barbara Brandt

Whole Life Economics: Revaluing Daily Life. Philadelphia: New Society Publishers, 1995.

Anja Anjelica Chan

Women and Sexual Harassment: A Practical Guide to the Legal Protections of Title VII and the Hostile Environment Claim. New York: Haworth Press, 1993.

Hillary Rodham Clinton

It Takes a Village: And Other Lessons Children Teach Us. New York: Simon & Schuster, 1995.

Faye J. Crosby

Juggling: The Unexpected Advantages of Balancing Career and Home for Women and Their Families. New York: Free Press, 1993.

George E. Curry, ed.

The Affirmative Action Debate. Reading, MA: Addison-Wesley, 1996.

Bette J. Dickerson

African American Single Mothers: Understanding Their Lives and Families. Newbury Park, CA: Sage, 1994.

Lorraine Dusky

Still Unequal: The Shameful Truth About Women and Justice in America. New York: Crown Publishers, 1996.

Kathryn Edin and
Laura Lein

Making Ends Meet: How Single Mothers Survive Welfare and Low-Wage Work. New York: Russell Sage Foundation, 1997.

Lynne Eisaguirre

Sexual Harassment: A Reference Handbook. Santa Barbara, CA: ABC-CLIO, 1993.

Diane E. Eyer	*Mother-Infant Bonding: A Scientific Fiction.* New Haven, CT: Yale University Press, 1992.
Warren Farrell	*The Myth of Male Power.* New York: Simon & Schuster, 1993.
Federal Glass Ceiling Commission	*Good for Business: Making Full Use of the Nation's Human Capital.* Washington, DC: U.S. Department of Labor, March 1995.
Linda Bird Francke	*Ground Zero: The Gender Wars in the Military.* New York: Simon & Schuster, 1997.
Judith Frankel, ed.	*The Employed Mother and the Family Context.* New York: Springer Publishing, 1993.
Lucia Albino Gilbert	*Two Careers / One Family: The Promise of Gender Equality.* Newbury Park, CA: Sage, 1993.
Rose Glickman	*Daughters of Feminists.* New York: St. Martin's Press, 1993.
Steven Goldberg	*Why Men Rule: A Theory of Male Dominance.* Chicago: Open Court, 1993.
Linda Gordon	*Pitied but Not Entitled: Single Mothers and the History of Welfare.* New York: Free Press, 1994.
Kent Greenawalt	*Fighting Words: Individuals, Communities, and Liberties of Speech.* Princeton, NJ: Princeton University Press, 1995.
Morley Gunderson	*Comparable Worth and Gender Discrimination: An International Perspective.* Geneva, Switzerland: International Labor Office, 1994.
Anita M. Harris	*Broken Patterns: Professional Women and the Quest for a New Feminine Identity.* Detroit: Wayne State University Press, 1995.
Sharon Hays	*The Cultural Contradictions of Motherhood.* New Haven, CT: Yale University Press, 1996.
Sheila B. Kamerman	*Starting Right: How America Neglects Its Youngest Children and What We Can Do About It.* New York: Oxford University Press, 1995.
Mary P. Koss et al.	*No Safe Haven: Male Violence Against Women at Home, at Work, and in the Community.* Washington, DC: American Psychological Association, 1994.
Anne Levy and Michelle Paludi	*Workplace Sexual Harassment.* Upper Saddle River, NJ: Prentice-Hall, 1996.
Rhonda Mahony	*Kidding Ourselves: Breadwinning, Babies, and Bargaining Power.* New York: BasicBooks, 1995.
Sherri Matteo	*American Women in the Nineties: Today's Critical Issues.* Boston: Northeastern University Press, 1993.

Bonnie J. Miller-McLemore	*Also a Mother: Work and Family as Theological Dilemma.* Nashville: Abingdon Press, 1994.
Gwendolyn Mink	*The Wages of Motherhood: Maternalist Social Policy, Race, and the Political Origins of Women's Inequality in the Welfare State.* Ithaca, NY: Cornell University Press, 1995.
Cynthia Negry	*Gender, Time, and Reduced Work.* Albany: State University of New York Press, 1993.
Valerie Polakow	*Lives on the Edge: Single Mothers and Their Children in the Other America.* Chicago: University of Chicago Press, 1993.
The Presidential Commission on the Assignment of Women in the Armed Forces	*Report to the President.* Washington, DC: GPO, November 15, 1992.
Kathleen Kelley Reardon	*They Don't Get It, Do They? Communication in the Workplace—Closing the Gap Between Women and Men.* Boston: Little, Brown, 1995.
Barbara F. Reskin and Irene Padavic	*Women and Men at Work.* Thousand Oaks, CA: Pine Forge Press, 1994.
Steven Rhoads	*Incomparable Worth: Pay Equity Meets the Market.* New York: Cambridge University Press, 1993.
Suzanne Uttaro Samuels	*Gender Equality in the Workplace.* Madison: University of Wisconsin Press, 1995.
Virginia E. Schein	*Working from the Margins: Voices of Mothers in Poverty.* Ithaca, NY: ILR Press, 1995.
Beth Anne Shelton	*Women, Men, and Time: Gender Differences in Paid Work, Housework, and Leisure.* New York: Greenwood Press, 1992.
Linda Jean Shepherd	*Lifting the Veil: The Feminine Face of Science.* Boston: Shambhala, 1993.
Elaine Sorensen	*Comparable Worth: Is It a Worthy Policy?* Princeton, NJ: Princeton University Press, 1994.
Judith Hicks Stiehm, ed.	*It's Our Military Too! Women and the U.S. Military.* Philadelphia: Temple University Press, 1996.
Joan Kennedy Taylor	*Women's Issues: Feminism, Classical Liberalism, and the Future.* Stanford, CA: Hoover Institution, 1993.
U.S. House Committee on Armed Services, Subcommittee on Military Personnel and Compensation	*Women in the Military: The Tailhook Affair and the Problem of Sexual Harassment.* Washington, DC: GPO, September 14, 1992.
Gregory L. Vitsica	*Fall from Glory.* New York: Simon & Schuster, 1996.

| Rick Weissbourd | The Vulnerable Child: What Really Hurts America's Children and What We Can Do About It. Reading, MA: Addison-Wesley, 1996. |

Linda Witt, Karen M. Paget, and Glenna Mathews — Running as a Woman: Gender and Power in American Politics. New York: Free Press, 1993.

Naomi Wolf — Fire with Fire: The New Female Power and How It Will Change the Twenty-First Century. New York: Random House, 1993.

Jean Zimmerman — Tailspin: Women at War in the Wake of Tailhook. New York: Doubleday, 1995.

David Zucchino — Myth of the Welfare Queen. New York: Scribner's, 1997.

INDEX

Abzug, Bella, 138
Adarand v. Pena, 96
affirmative action
  breeds discrimination, 97
  debate is over group vs.
    individual rights, 100
  opponents focus on race, 90
  should be results-based, 94
  con, 100
Albright, Madeleine, 77, 78
American Journal of Public Health, 32
Anita Hill–Clarence Thomas
  hearings, 107
  EEOC cases filed since, 114
Army Times, 158
Aspin, Les, 162
Atkins, Carol, 108
Atlantic Monthly, 36
authority
  sex differences in, 49
Awake!, 109

Barnes v. Train, 114
Barnett, Rosalind C., 21
Barry, John, 131
Biddle, Jeff, 98
Billingsley, K.L., 153
birthrates
  are rising, 36
Bleckley, Jessica, 119
Bowlby, John, 37, 42
Brave New World (Huxley), 38
Bravo, Ellen, 109
Brazelton, T. Berry, 41
Breslow, Marc, 25
Brown, Helen Gurley, 109, 110
Brown v. Board of Education, 162
Buckingham Computer Services,
  116–17
businesses
  assumptions about costs to
    employ women, 55–56
  defending against sexual
    harassment is costly, 116–17
  flexibility for working mothers
    in, 82
  male-owned, receive majority of

public contracts, 93
women-owned, numbers of are
  growing, 76, 99
Business Insurance, 116

Cadick, Jerry R., 165
California Civil Rights Initiative
  (CCRI), 58
Caputo, Patricia, 81
Carlucci, Frank, 142
Cassedy, Ellen, 109
Castro, Ida L., 67
Charen, Mona, 62
Chavez, Linda, 17
chief executive officers (CEOs)
  female, among Fortune 1000
    companies, 65
  views of, on glass ceiling, 66–67
Christensen, Kathleen, 82
Citadel, 93
Civil Rights Act of 1964, 77, 90,
  110
Clagett, John, 167
Coats, Dan, 131
Colburn, Claudia, 130
Conservative Chronicle, 62, 99
Crittenden, Danielle, 85
Crosby, Faye J., 42

"Dan Quayle Was Right"
  (Whitehead), 36
Davis, Paul O., 157
Department of Labor, U.S., 61
Department of the Treasury, U.S.,
  53
DiGiovacchino, Paul, 66
discrimination
  against mothers, 82
  sexual, 55
    affirmative action breeds, 97
    customer preferences as
      grounds for, 56
    EEOC complaints of, 55
diversity specialists
  portray women as victims, 74
divorce, 18
DuBois, Ellen, 96